GROWING OLDER WITHOUT GROWING OLD

GROWING OLDER WITHOUT GROWING OLD

◆

THE ART OF AGEING

Compiled by Umberto Vasari and Peter Abbey

iUniverse, Inc.
New York Lincoln Shanghai

GROWING OLDER WITHOUT GROWING OLD
THE ART OF AGEING

iUniverse books may be ordered through booksellers or by contacting:

iUniverse
2021 Pine Lake Road, Suite 100
Lincoln, NE 68512
www.iuniverse.com
1-800-Authors (1-800-288-4677)

Original art work by Mr. Hank A. Cepeda

ISBN-13: 978-0-595-38261-3 (pbk)
ISBN-13: 978-0-595-82632-2 (ebk)
ISBN-10: 0-595-38261-4 (pbk)
ISBN-10: 0-595-82632-6 (ebk)

Printed in the United States of America

This book is published by
The Education Foundation
in cooperation with
Hagakure Press

To
Marcus Tullius Cicero
(106—43 B.C.)
for
writing the standard on the subject
De Senectute
(On Old Age)

"An old age in need of self-improvement is unenviable."
De Senectute [44 B.C.], Book VI

Contents

A. GUIDANCE: SPIRITUAL /MEDICAL/ SOCIAL

B. COPING: SOME STORIES AND SONGS ABOUT AGEING

C. TESTIMONIALS: LEARNING THE ART OF AGEING

Growing Older Without Growing Old: The Art of Ageing

The book is titled *Growing Older Without Growing Old: The Art of Ageing*. If you are fortunate and do not die early by accident or disease, you will become old in this century which will produce more aged people and centenarians than any other century in human history.

To get to old age is one task; to make it valuable is another. This book assumes you have or will want to become old and, more importantly, you desire to find some purposeful role in your being old. This book is meant to help you but it may not. It depends, of course, on you. That is why we call it "The Art of Ageing."

This book is dedicated to Cicero and his *DE SENECTUTE* ("About Old Age") because many of us think his essay on the importance and benefits of being older remains the best of the lot.

This book increases the lot by presenting various viewpoints from a variety of highly opinionated elders from three continents: Europe, America and Asia.

Mr. Richard Jones, the British novelist, in the first essay, *Age and I*, tells us about his epiphany when typecast as "old" and then proceeds to reflect on the social differences when a youth in Wales and the current benefits of being older in the United Kingdom.

Dr. Peter Abbey asks from Monaco how do we become old well and what of value do the experts tell us. He reviews the history and literature of ageing and acts as our escort, our psycho-pomp, guiding us through centuries of viewpoints about old age. He thereby also presents us with an extensive bibliography on a subject worth considering.

As both a university professor and a priest, Dr William A. Johnson reviews Cicero and his influence on Christianity before presenting Christianity's own perspective on old age, defined by its celebration of death, acceptance of suffering and promise of eternal life.

A practicing psychiatrist and a life-long Buddhist, Dr. Josef Kolenski, describes for us the many comforts elderly people can derive from this millennial-old religious philosophy.

Dr. Ralph N. Wharton is a university psychiatrist who gives us a mixture of classical Ciceronian maxims and modern case studies that educate and entertain us about being and behaving older.

From China, the renowned economist, Dr. Shuming Zhao and his associate, Dr. Huifang Yang, offer us suggestions about dealing with our individual ageing while they propose what China should do economically and socially to meet the vast problems their nation faces as the population ages after decades of the one child per family policy.

Then you are presented some whimsy about old age. A Brothers Grimm fairy tale is coupled with two popular songs and some cartoons with an attitude as various examples of how to manage the so-called "golden years." Mr. Ervin Drake, the noted American composer, and the veteran British actor Mr. Clive Dunn offer us two different pieces; Mr. Arnold Drake of graphic novel and X-Men fame gives us his comic viewpoint about being older.

Lastly, there are four different opinions about how to manage old age: Biblical, secular, artistic and philosophic.

Pope John Paul II in his 80th year wrote down "in a conversation" his own "deeper personal understanding of this phase of life...." He thought the elderly were the guardians of shared memory and are the special servants of God as the Bible and the writings of the Church Fathers verify: Old age has a place "in the mysterious plan of providence." He contrasts the ruin of old age in the Old Testament's *Ecclesiastes* with the promise of the resurrection in the New Testament of Luke, John and Paul's *Romans*. He asks older people to live life serenely in the faithful knowledge that the elderly believer will be called "from life to life." The letter presents also his resolute opposition to euthanasia.

Mr. John Timperley, the British playwright, also writes in his mature years but answers the same question of why live to be old quite differently. He remembers his roots and settles for an acceptance of a humane life: "we are what we are." Instead of Biblical citations, he prefers popular songs and chooses to live and to die with vibrant hope and resonant love.

The American Broadway actress and singer Ms. Wynne Miller and the Austrian portrait painter Count Rudolf Bernatschke offer us a dialogue between Music and Painting, reflecting that life can be happily lived as a continuance and development of one's art which becomes then a dynamic definition for older age.

Then to Asia for a neo-traditional Chinese viewpoint on the discipline and self-awareness required for enjoying an old age. Professor Cao Qingyang argues that a philosophy combining proper diet, daily exercise, mental activity and stress management are the bases for a happy longevity, "the harvest season when aged people should recreate brilliance…from continuous effort and creativity." 5000 years of assurance are here.

You have with *Growing Older But Not Growing Old* contemporary, international answers to the question of how to age well—and also many encouragements to age artfully.

This book is the first of a series that invites authors from various countries and cultures around the world to address ageing as an international, national and a personal issue. Notice that we have chosen to use the British spelling of "ageing" in this book.

Hagakure Press is thanked for its collaborative assistance and The Education Foundation for its gracious support in producing this book. The noted graphic artist Mr. Hank A. Cepeda drew the cover and the pictures introducing each chapter.

Appreciation is also given to Dr. Thomas G. Voss for suggesting the idea and inviting many of the authors who are participants in this book.

Profits from the sale of this book are given to international charities that assist the elderly.

Dr. Umberto Vasari
General Editor
The Academy
Rome

PREFACE

THE SURPRISE OF AGEING

AGE AND I

I first grasped that growing old might not be as simple as I had thought when, at some point in 1977, I read two ageist comments that impressed me so much that I copied them into my diary. The first, from an advert for *Playboy* in *The New York Times*, gave the opinion of one Dawson Wallace: "To me, a travel bargain is someplace the old folks don't go. I'm willing to pay a lot for that." The second appeared in a Richmond magazine (I was living in Virginia at the time) and was about a weathergirl called Cindy. It seemed that to sportsman Jim Granger Cindy was a "delicate little pixie" who "bubbles on the air. People like her. Old guys about 50 always tell me they love Cindy." Old guys of about 50? That was a shock. I was 50 and had never thought of myself as old but, it was clear, other people did so and thought nothing of paying extra to be sure they were never in my company. So what did it mean? I questioned friends and colleagues and they tended not to take the remarks as seriously as I did. It could be, I was told, some disliked older- or old-people because they looked like the careworn men and women the young feared to become. It could also be that the elderly did not fit into the American cult of youth and, incapable of changing with fashion and new visions of the world, did not enhance the view. No theory for the hatred of the elderly was satisfactory and then came the question: What to do? The answer was nothing at all and I decided that such ideas about age were an American attitude and had nothing in common with the ones I had grown up with. So I copied out the quotes and went on living as before.

Yet this was new to me as I had no fixed ideas about age and old people. They were there; they were, in some cases, friends and neighbors and there was no reason why one should avoid or fear them. I don't think I had ever met any older people as a type. A social type—calling for special reactions and avoidance and when the guy in the ad boasted he would pay extra to be away from old people did that mean all people of my age? Or just a specially disfavored few? The fact remains that I had never heard old people criticized as a group or class. They were everywhere in my native country because people stayed put in their communities and grew old alongside their children and children's children.

Generally speaking, in 1930s rural Wales, people carried on working as long as possible and it was rare to know someone who was in every sense "retired" because the country people believed in the value of work and seemed not to have the notion that, at a certain point, society owed them a prolonged vacation. My grandfathers on both sides worked until they died. This was a period before the culture of moving into retirement homes or to retirement towns and villages.

Ours was a mixed community, solidly nonconformist in religion (Calvinistic Methodist, to be exact) a meeting point of dairy farming and the houses of professionals who offices were in the neighboring town. Between these two groups were those working in the service industries and a handful who had made their lives and money in London and had returned to their native region to enjoy a quiet and respectable life of gardening and churchgoing as advocated by the society they had worked in. These were the truly "retired" people in the present-day sense.

The richest local family owned a brewery and these were the folks who took overseas vacations and also provided the first instance of departure for a retiree's town on the south coast of England. There are several resorts and regions favoured by the elderly from the stretch of towns in Sussex, known as Costa Geriatrica, to the fishing villages of Cornwall. Our neighbor's choice was Bournemouth, half way between the two and, we were told, a place blessed with a symphony orchestra and a fine art gallery. It was understood, by those who bothered to listen, that one needed a cultural life to space out the time spent in the garden or drinking coffee on the pier. The departure from the norm created some speculation and it was thought that the family had gone to Bournemouth because cousins had already moved there. Whatever the reason, once these folks moved away they never returned.

The majority of the farming families enjoyed the active support of the older generation and there were always tasks that older people could perform and did so willingly. Their continued presence in the community meant there were cross-generational relationships. When I started at the local infant's school I was reminded by the devout and marvelous woman who taught the first years that she had known my father and my mother's younger brother as pupils. Miss Clark was near the end of her career and enthusiasm for her skill as a teacher united the generations. Later on, I moved to the town grammar school and this was the beginning of the change of gear about time: My timetable was laid down by social practice, secondary school led to the world of work or, possibly, to university or training college and we lived social timetables. When the war broke out, there was conscription or national service. One was serving society and I don't think I ever imagined I would develop a special attitude to growing old. It was in the way of things to grow old like other people and, with passing years, one became aware of pension rights, putting money aside for marriage, buying a house, educating children and, eventually, for assured comfort in old age, the economic power to help younger members of the family. Everyone who was in work was a member of the national social security system which laid down what pension one could expect. People spoke of the desirability of getting jobs with good pensions and everyone was free, if means were available, to take out a private pension scheme in addition to the national one. About this time one heard adventurous spirits claiming that they despised those who sought job and pensions security on the grounds that life was meant to be an adventure. This point of view is never heard today at a time when successive governments have added to the basic financial structure so that, at this time, pensioners are entitled to a once a year payment for heating costs and those over 75 are not obliged to pay the annual fee for the right to watch television. In London there is a significant contribution to the financial wellbeing of the over-60s: they receive a freedom pass which allows the holder to travel by train, subway and bus for nothing apart from the morning rush-hours. This zone extends for about 15 miles from the city centre and, given the high cost of public transport in London, is a valuable bonus.

Apart from changing financial values there have been changing fashions and expectations. Stage by stage the cult of youth became commonplace: Everyone needed to look younger than one was and the concept of "the grey pound" was born so that the elderly found themselves wooed by special services, and their own press. One of the great commercial successes is the magazine "SAGA" whose pages are filled with adverts directed at the older sector—everything from appropriate footwear and clothes to vacations, cruises and tours especially geared for an older and more discriminating clientele. "SAGA" has established its own public services from radio stations to travel agencies. The magazine makes growing old a new form of adventure and its readers are encouraged to be positive at all times.

Although the longer-living seniors have created problems for the health service and residential homes the incredible boom in property prices, common throughout Britain, has given older people the freedom to realize untold sums of money for helping the younger generation and for pleasure. A new idea that helped the elderly is equity release whereby property owners over 60 can raise a mortgage which is only repaid when the mortgagees die. The general picture is now encouraging, and there may even be a change in the attitude to growing old. To a certain extent social formulae define a modern human being's progress from early years to age. Social usage lays down the dates for marriage, buying one's first house. And one finds that these big events take place against a background of other people's expectations. The newly liberated older person has greater freedom of action although the more responsible still accept that they are involved in the health and concerns of their friends and family. Yet even at the stage when one visits elderly relatives in hospitals and retirement homes one never truly formulates a self-contained policy for one's old age. One just hopes that when the testing time comes one will have the will and the means to meet the challenge of incapacity.

This is the time of the most brutal lessons: Nothing you have ever thought or discussed with others can make the arrival of old age seem anything but a violation of one's rights as an ordinary human being. It doesn't help at all that people discuss ageing, and one picks up bits of advice on how to lessen the problems, but nobody pretends that the onset of the worst aspects of old age are anything but a severe test of one's patience and courage with the added discomfort of accepting that others see you in this state as a burden and a drag. Some might ask: Did you not have any projects reserved for later years? And my answer is none at all. Had we ever thought we might move to another area or a smaller house or into a retirement home and the answer is negative. We can't think of any place we'd rather be than the district in south-west London where we live at this time. I don't know that I ever thought that my old age would be so comfortable, so lacking in personal tension apart from natural concerns about health and possible incapacity. I and my wife have maintained our interests and enthusiasms and enjoy our friends, our travels and successes of the younger generation. All this suggests that there has never been a time when the mass of the elderly population has been as well-established and as at home in their skins as this one. Of course, this security and comfort must make the fate of the elderly in less fortunate countries seem like a reproach whether we are touched by the poverty-stricken old women selling small items in the streets near the subway stations in St. Petersburg and Moscow or the despairing survivors of the Indian Ocean earthquake; and these are the occasions when we examine what might be considered our own smugness and repent.

There is, it has to be said, one feature of old age that no amount of foresight or hard thought can prepare for: The loss of those one has known and loved for years. All address books become peopled by ghosts and the amusing, helpful and enlivening friends and relatives who were only a telephone call away have gone ahead into the great silence and we are left trying to work out how we can reconcile ourselves to their absence.

—Richard Jones

About Ageing:
Opinions and Insights
From Cicero to Simone:
De Senectute to La Vieillesse
(A Review of the Literature about
Ageing)

The National Institute on Aging in Washington, D.C. and other authorities tell us:

There are over 65 million people in the USA over 50 years of age.

In 2005, 38 million "Boomers" were 50 or older;

Over 50s number 35% of the current population,

But they have 75% of the financial assets and 59% of discretionary funds;

An estimated 41 trillion dollars will pass to the next generation by 2052.

In 1900, 4 percent of the American population was over 65 years old; today it is 12 %.

By 2035, the over 65 population in the USA will be 20%; Social Security will be in deficit by 2018.

Life expectancy in 1900 was 47 years; today it is 77; by 2050 it will be 83

At 65, a male American can expect 17 more years of life;

And a female 7 years more; today 4 of 5 centenarians are female.

Alzheimer's disease afflicts 3% of Americans ages 65-74; but 47% past age 85.

By 2050, it is estimated there will be 600,000 centenarians, ten times as many as today.

For the first time in history, there will be more people over 65 than under age 15 in the world.

Most Americans asked how long they would like to live chose an average age of 87; 25% said 100 or older; and only 7% opted to live "forever."

Like the rest of the world, America is an ageing nation. Yet many people think America is not a place to be an old person. It is a nation devoted to the cult of youth and beauty and old age is rarely discussed and never welcomed. There is no fruition or purpose in becoming old in America. Rules and responsibilities are legislated or assumed for the young and the middle aged, but for the old, there are only the expectations of physical illness, social loneliness, mental deprivation and then final oblivion.

As one incisive author, Dr. Robert N. Butler, asked in a 1970s book *Why Survive Growing Old in America?* Indeed America is a hard place to be old, despite government assistance with such programs as Social Security and Medicaid/Medicare. There is little tolerance for being old; there is no publicly accepted social purpose for the elderly; there is no recognition of the value or merit of old people. At best, those elderly who look younger are saluted and those who remain lively are congratulated. It is an insulting paradigm, but one practiced commonly in America and many western societies. Aged westerners might consider relocating to Asia, Africa or the Middle East where their traditions and religions promote old people as national resources to be given respect and care.

Yet the 21st century will be the first "Silver Century" in history having more old people than young. The world will change and you will change it since you will become or are already old in this century.

But, first, when do we get old? Hippocrates said old age began at 56; Solon thought "full measure" 70; Aristotle claimed after 50; Dante thought it started at 45; in the United States, it is officially at age 65

If the 17th century discovered childhood as an important part of life and society, then the 20th century discovered ageing. The first International Gerontology Congress was held in 1950. The US Congress passed "The Older Americans Act" in 1965, its first major elder law after Social Security in 1935 that pegged 65 as old age. The first American book about ageing was published in 1922 by G. Stanley Hall.

The early 20th century discovered an interest in the ageing population because it was doubling every thirty years. The medical field of geriatrics officially began in the United States in 1909 when Dr. Nascher of New York City founded "The Society of Geriatry." Gerontology developed at the same time but differs in that it does not inquire about the pathology but only about the process of growing old.

American and Western society is now growing older. The approaching retirement of the 1943-1960 generation, called "Baby Boomers," will add to the already mostly retired 1925-1942 "Silent Generation." But the Boomers seem also to have no strategy or philosophy about their purpose or role in being older people. America has not focused on old age before; it will in the near future.

Where should we look to find the meaning and significance of old age? Perhaps we need to go back to the time when old age was rare since life was short and often brutish. Why not begin with the Bible?

The Bible does credit old age with virtue, wisdom and strength (Lev. 19:32; Job 12:12; Ps. 92:14-15); and God grants his chosen the blessing of longevity (Ps. 90:10): Abraham leaves his home at 75 to become the "father of many nations";

Moses was nearly 80 when he led the Israelites out of Egypt and would spend 40 years more leading them; Eleazar was 90 when he died valiantly for his faith (2 Macc. 6:24ff); the prophetess Anna was 84 when she saw the infant Jesus (Lk. 2:37-38) who would prove a major exception.

The Bible offers old age insurance to the godly. There is of course the commandment: "Honor your father and mother, so your days in the land…may be long (Ex 20:12; Dt.5:16). And there are more assurances: (The pious old) shall outwork the young (Is. 40:30-31); be renewed in strength (Is. 40:31; Ps.103; 5); and "bear fruit even in old age, vigorous and sturdy shall they be." (Ps. 92:15) The Lord may save the best for last (Jn. 2:10) and thereby proclaims the opposite of "old" is not "young" but "new" through faith. A cyclical generational covenant is made with the young in the fourth commandment—"Honor thy father and mother: that thy days may be long…." (Ex. 20:12) These thoughts are comforting until one recalls God's seemingly irrational cruelty to the elderly in His demands on Abraham for Isaac, His denial of Moses into the Promised Land and His wager about Job.

But there is another remarkable and special elder blessing found in the first chapter of First Kings. When the aged King David becomes cold, he is given warmth by the young virgin Abishag, a Shunammite:
"A damsel (who) was very fair, and cherished the king, and ministered to him: but the king knew her not." (1Kg.1: 4) God doth indeed work his wonders in strange and mysterious ways to behold.

If we cannot find a comprehensive elder role in the Bible, maybe a purposeful perspective for ageing can be found in the other ancient cultures?

In China, Confucius defined the harmonious society by designating the oldest man to be the unquestioned family patriarch to whom all must be obedient. He has this authority until he reached 70. Then he should relinquish his power and prepare for a proper death. Lao-Tze, the other principal wise man of Asia, said this preparation for death should begin at 60 with an asceticism that would allow a long life and a final apotheosis to the "ranks of the spirits."

Such filial obligations gave old men a place in China for millennia. However, that ancient social code is no longer honored after Maoism, materialism and the current 4-2-1 family of four grandparents, two parents and one child. These last decades have placed the old Chinese ways upside down, making children often "little emperors."

How about Egypt? An extent Egyptian writing of some 4500 years ago declares: "old age is the worst of misfortunes that can afflict a man."

What about those noble Greeks and Romans?

In Greece, Homer's Nestor in the *Iliad* is the aged wise counselor, but his elderly fragility allows Ulysees to become the champion, just as in Troy Hector similarly surpasses Priam. Aristophanes mocks the old in *The Clouds* and in *Lysistrata* and Sophocles' aged protagonist in *Oedipus at Colonus* is a blind, wretched wanderer: "When a man is old, the light of his reason goes out, action becomes useless and he has unmeaning cares." (Sophocles was said to be 89 when he finished that play.) However, both Sparta and Athens gave their old men significant ruling powers and those societies did greatly flourish.

Plato as a young man wrote in *The Republic*, Book I, under the character of Cephalus: "As age blunts one's enjoyment of physical pleasures, one's desire is for the things of the intellect...." Plato as Socrates muses that one learns from the old and Cephalus adds: "Old age gives us peace and liberation (from the passions)." Then he leaves the symposium. In his *Republic*, Plato has Socrates say old men should preside over the magistrates and the young from ages 50 to 75. Later, when 80, Plato in his *Laws* argued for filial respect and support for parents and family elders. But Aristotle later disagreed and wrote old age began after 50 and in his *Politics* and *Ethics* viewed old age as a time of deterioration and decrepitude. He suggested old men become officially a kind of priestly caste where they can be of no bother but of some possible assistance as advisors, something like the earlier Chinese views and those found later in the 17th century in the famous Japanese samurai handbook called *Hagakure*.

The Romans are also in conflict toward ageing. Juvenal in his satires portrays old age as a time of sadness, infirmity and obsolescence; Pliny the Elder thought an early death was "nature's greatest blessing" rather than bearing an old age; Horace, Martial and Ovid portray old age as a time of bitterness and sterility; Plautus mocks rich old fools; Seneca at 61 in his *Letters* writes about old age as the fine and fitting time of life to free the soul; and then there was the thoughtful Cicero whom we review later.

If not the ancients, perhaps we should look to the Christian Age and to the Renaissance.

The Christian Age seems a very dark and sad time for old people. St. Isidore of Seville, as an example, noted in the 7th century that old age began at 50 and was called "old age" since the body "shrinks" and "people's wits fail and they dote." The monasteries, convents and the local rulers often cared for the few aged under the rubric of Christian charity. Usually the Middle Ages portrayed the aged body at best as a decaying instrument for the flowering soul. An exception could be literary heroes who often were long lived as in *La Mort d'Arthur* where Arthur is over 100, and Lancelot, Guenivere and the rest are very frisky at 60 to 80; however, both Boccaccio and Chaucer tell sad tales of January-May marriages which have very bad results.

The Renaissance generally overlooked old age and preferred to display the beauties of youth. (Rembrandt and da Vinci are the only major exceptions: They painted some old people with definite character.) Like most artists, Michelangelo and da Vinci portrayed mostly youth and strength and wrote they were greatly vexed by their ageing. Shakespeare's *King Lear*, often seen as a study of a self-inflicted foolish old age resulting in destitution and death, has been read also as a tragedy telling the sad ending of all humanity condemned to a useless and fruitless old age. (It is interesting that *Oedipus at Colonus* and *King Lear* are the only two major western plays with aged main characters.) Shakespeare in *As You Like It* has Jacques describe the seven ages of man with old age as "the last scene of all—sans teeth, sans eyes, sans taste, sans everything." Goethe in *Faust* described old age as a time of unfulfilled regret and hopeful reincarnation. However, western society's "old age problem" did not really surface until the 19th century when the Industrial Age allowed a significant population to survive beyond 50.

Within this short survey of the pre-modern culture of ageing, Cicero deserves more specific attention since he is most comprehensive and instructive.

Less than three generations ago it was common for many American high school students to study Latin.

In the fifties, high school students still read Cicero since he was considered understandable and moral in comparison to Ovid, Lucretius or Juvenal. Some teenagers even read Cicero's *De Senectute* since it was considered easy Latin for beginners. However, the sundry benefits of growing old Cicero argued so cogently escaped all of those students. In the early 21st century, many of those students are now superannuated and should re-read *De Senectute* and the rising "Boomer" generation might be well advised to be introduced to Cicero's philosophy about the art of ageing.

Cicero was 62 years old when he wrote the essay, about one year before he was assassinated by order of the Second Triumvirate to placate Mark Antony, the butt of Cicero's *Phillipics*. The essay was dedicated to Atticus, his old friend, who was three years older than Cicero.

Cicero had then time to write. He was still mourning the death of his beloved daughter Tullia; he was out of office and out of political favor with Octavius, Lepidus and especially Mark Antony whose junta now ruled Rome after Julius Caesar's death. Much of *De Senectute* can be read as a treatise on the need to have old wise men in the Senate in order to protect the state: Cicero wrote also to keep his job.

Classical scholars say Cicero was an idealist who managed successfully to attain all the responsible civic positions in Rome from quaestor to consul. Yet he failed in the end due to his Republican values and his defense of the Roman constitution. They say he viewed mankind as living in a rational universe within a preordained natural law that was the measure of all human laws; however, he practically adopted a moderate skepticism founded on his own brand of flexible, adaptable stoicism. In both his political and literary lives, he equated rhetoric with the art of thinking well and speaking well. And that he did.

In *De Senectute*, Cicero has his character Laelius ask his own alter ego, the 80 year-old Cato:
"I have never noticed that you find it wearisome to be old. That is different from other old men, who claim to find old age a heavier burden than Mount Etna itself.
Cato replies: You are praising me for something that, in my opinion, has not been a very difficult achievement. A person who lacks the means, within himself, to live a good and happy life will find any period of his existence wearisome. But rely for life's blessings on your own resources, and you will not take a gloomy view of any of the inevitable consequences of nature's laws. Everyone hopes to

attain an advanced age; yet when it comes they all complain!...I regard nature as the best guide: I follow and obey her as a divine being."

Laelius adds: "We hope and desire to live long enough to see old age. Could you not tell us how its oncoming can be made endurable? If you can, you will be doing us a great favor."

Like Cephalus in Plato's *Republic*, Book One, over two hundred years earlier, Cicero's Cato suggests that "the study and practice of decent and enlightened living" is the best preparation for old age.

He goes on to illustrate his case by questioning the four assumptions about growing old: the weakening of the mind; the weakening of the body; the loss of sensual and physical pleasures; and the fear of death.

Old age should not take us away from active work. Remember, says Cato, Plato before he died at 81 still wrote treatises; Isocrates at 94 finished writing a book and lived five more years; Gorgias, the sophist, died at 107. Sophocles who left the world at 90 in his old age composed *Oedipus at Colonus* and the aged Socrates learned to play the lyre. He notes that "some people never stop learning, however old they are.... Old age should not be feared for weakening the mind."

As for the weakening of the body, Cato says" exercise and self-control enable a man to preserve a good deal of his former strength after he has become old."

But are there any pleasures in ageing? Cato (as earlier Sophocles and Socrates) answers that one benefit is the removal of "lustful pleasures" which torment youth and middle age: "Let sensuality be present and a good life becomes impossible." It is replaced by better pursuits: for example, the joys of conversation and friendship. "When its campaigns of sex, ambition, rivalry, quarreling, and all the other passions are ended, the human spirit returns to live within itself—and is well off."

Cato urges a proper occupation for old age—the consolation of farming whereby one may realize the fruits of his labor and leave something for posterity to enjoy. (Thomas Jefferson agreed when he planted his trees at Monticello.) It is an occupation of value and beauty and within the capabilities of an old age.

As for death—the fourth objection to becoming old—there is either oblivion or the eternal life of the soul—there is no third option. Cato opts for the latter and argues there should be no fear of our end in either option. "When life's last act, old age, has become wearisome, when we have had enough, the time has come to go."

Cicero as Cato wrote: "I do not regret that I have lived, since I have so lived that I think I was not born in vain, and I quit life as if it were an inn, not a home."

It has been argued after Cicero's *De Senectute*, all other books about ageing are but variations on his four themes. The Middle Ages and Renaissance agreed and characterized Cicero as a great mentor and prophet in politics, logic, rhetoric and learning as well as a guide for ageing well.

To explore that theory, and to continue our search for meaning in old age, we now turn to the moderns to see what they may offer us by way of a suitable role for growing old—or what they may add to Cicero's analysis.

There are three major kinds of contemporary books about ageing written for those who are ageing. I call this modern genre "Missionary Sermons for the Ageing." They are usually self-help books for people past fifty. One type, often written by physicians, is about achieving an old age and I describe that segment as "The Longevity Merchants"; another is collections of stories and essays by various older people, often celebrities, that I name the "Elders as Mentors" series; the third kind offers a singular strategy or a philosophy for accepting ageing and I call that genre the "Elders as Prophets" series. (This last category has a subsection entitled "The Minor Prophets.")

The Longevity Merchants

To capitalize on this generation's growing interest in the living long lives, various diet and exercise books have been published the last years.

The current literature on ageing is mostly by medical people who argue diet, exercise, moderation, attitude and genes are the five keys to achieve longevity. From the best selling, *Age Free Zone* (1999) by Barry Sears, Ph.D.; to *Live Now, Age Later: Proven Ways to Slow Down the Clock* (2000) by Isadore Rosenfeld M.D., through *Longevity Code* (2001) by Zorba Paster, M.D., to *Aging with*

Grace (2001) by David Snowden M.D, to *Asian Longevity Secrets* (2003) by Ping Wu, M.D. and *Anti-Aging Solution (Five Steps to Looking and Feeling Young)* (2004) by Vincent Giampapa, M.D. et al; to even a *Living Longer for Dummies* (2001) by Walter M. Bortz M.D.; to *Aging Well* by George E. Vaillant M.D. (2002) (predicated on Eric Erickson's eight stages of life, the author tells us that positive, successful ageing is based especially on the elderly embracing "generactivity."); and *Healthy Aging* (2005) by the noted medical guru Andrew Weil, M.D.(his book focuses on preventing or minimizing the impact of age related illnesses but also offers some practical advice to elders—e.g., "...don't forget to wear decent clothing. It is not good to go around shabbily dressed." [p.218]).

There are two exceptions to this genre. One of them is the readable and interesting *Successful Aging*, by John Rowe M.D. and Robert Kahn, Ph.D., funded by the MacArthur Foundation and based on their scientific study in 1998. The book statistically disproved many of the myths and prejudices about ageing (e.g., only 5% of people over 65 have debilitating illnesses) and shows old age is not necessarily a time of decrepitude. They suggest weight training, good nutrition and vitamins. Mental abilities, especially cognitive, will lessen, but it is a varied problem and often partly due to society's prejudice, Ageism.

Indeed "older men and women retain enough reserve capacity for meaningful and satisfying life, and for independence." (p.142.). However, they find: "In short by any available measure, older men and women are an underutilized productive resource." (p. 188). The report argues that the nation should become an "experimenting society," emulating Japan with its Silver Manpower Centers, allowing capable retired workers to find job placements, and urges a better integration of older Americans into our productive society.

Rowe and Kahn like Cicero offer gardening as a wonderful activity for the elderly since it puts them in real and spiritual contact with life and the future. They devote only two pages to elder sexuality and include Cicero's citation of Sophocles' reported delight in outgrowing sexual passion and the 1953 Kinsey Report, suggesting there are various forms of affectionate intimacy. There is very little about elder sexuality in the moderns. They all seem to heed Cicero's dictum or find the idea abhorrent.

Cicero does refer to various people both real and mythical as examples and as metaphors for his arguments. But rarely do Rowe and Kahn engage in stories from the aged, unlike so many others.

The other exception to the books about longevity and its potions is Dr. Robert N. Butler's *Why Survive? Being Old In America.* It was published in 1975 and reprinted in 2002 by Johns Hopkins Press. After three decades it proves sometimes dated, but it is never dull and always provocative.

Butler is blunt and focused. He begins: "Old age is often a tragedy…. At best, the living old are treated as if they were half dead." (p.xi) "What are an individual's chances for a 'good' old age in America, with satisfying years and a dignified death? Unfortunately, none too good." (p.2) "[It is]…a time of life with nothing to recommend it." (p.402). He portrays well and footnotes often the problems an elder American faces—in 1975: a deep rooted media culture insulting to the elderly, poor or non-existent pensions, inadequate housing, haphazard and unenforced legislation, prohibitive work rules, poor health services, various scams, unsuitable nursing homes and an isolated death. He calls this litany of abuse "Ageism" and makes it as a definitively pejorative a word as "Racism" and "Sexism."

He combines medical data, documented reports, a fine selection of poetry and prose and events from his own career as a psychiatrist to build a compelling case for the "absurdity" (nonsensical uselessness) of old age in America. (Happily he thinks Erik Erickson's terms "Generactivity" [versus Isolation] and "Integrity" [versus Despair], used often later in some books on ageing, such as those by Abigail Trafford and Betty Friedan [below], are from his experience useless, superficial and static identifications.)

After exploring in detail the failings and faults with the social infrastructures supposedly assisting the elderly, he opts for a real National Policy of Ageing to foster a liberated old age encouraging flexible retirements, an active and empowered old age, "life-cycle education," cultural integration, financial security (redesigned Social Security and Medicare systems—e.g., why not have Medicare guarantee a food allotment?) and overdue gerontological medical research and better geriatric services.

Dr. Butler argued for a complete overhaul of American thinking about the place and role of elders: "The tragedy of old age in America is that we have made absurdity all but inevitable. We have cheated ourselves. But we still have the possibility of making life a work of art." (p.422)

His book deservedly earned the Pulitzer Prize but did not change America.

About thirty years later, William H. Thomas M.D. attempted to answer Dr. Butler's question in *What are Old People For?* (2004). Thomas argues society must reverse the "unshakable equation of aging with decline" (p. 85) and recognize elders as "wisdom givers" and "legacy creators." We should create salaried "Shahbazim" (named for mythical caring birds) to serve as guardians, protectors and providers for the elderly (p.254 ff.). Also the aged should not be put into "rest homes," but rather into "Greenhouses," elder-topia communities, where their Shahbazim will encourage them to be "Being-doing" people and then they will have an elder life "made sweet indeed." (P. 313). (Alas, his book does not relate where aged Shahbazim should be housed; perhaps one may assume in "Shahbaz-kibbutzim.")

Elders as Mentors

There is a craze in elder books for printing "the wisdom of contemporaries," usually celebrities who have reached an older age. These books are composed of recollections, letters or interviews forming first person testimonials about being old. Celebrities and ordinary elders are solicited to share their experience by relating their own stories about growing elderly and being old both to entertain and to educate us.

The mentors series range from Willard Scott's *The Older the Fiddle, The Better the Tune* (2003); Connie Goldman's *The Ageless Spirit* (1992; reissued 2004); that redoubtable series senior entry, *Chicken Soup for the Golden Soul* (1999); Neenah Ellis *If I Live to be a Hundred* (2004); and the enjoyably eclectic *The Time of Your Life: Getting On with Getting On* (2002) compiled by the witty British author of children's books, John Burningham.

Scott solicited people like John Updike who wrote "one of the joys of being over sixty-five is that people have stopped trying to sell you insurance" and Monty Hall who proclaimed "feeling old age is an honor." NPR's Goldman asked Steve Allen, Eddie Albert, Jason Robards, Caesar Romero and many others to reminisce about their lives. Although the book is recently republished, many of the contributors are now deceased, thereby rendering their musings about living long and well somewhat questionable. The Chicken Soup franchise has many bowls. This book is for older people, those with the "Golden Soul," and should not be confused with *Chicken Soup for the Baseball Fan's Soul* (2001) or *Chicken Soup for the Nascar Soul* (2003). It is chock full of first hand, homey and "heartwarming" stories of ordinary folks' memories of memorable moments they now decode as templates. It is a reader's digest of articles and recollections. One of the chapters is "Fifty Reasons Why Older is Better" (e.g., "19. You don't have a bedtime."); another chapter is about the four brave US chaplains who drowned in 1943 while in early middle age. Perhaps this latter inclusion from a Rabbi who submitted it is to emphasize the importance of valor and courage through out life? Or perhaps they needed some more "heartwarming" filler?

Another NPR commentator, Neenah Ellis, has a book based on interviews with centenarians. It is her middle age exploration of those she once considered possibly aliens: Old people. Now she finds them curious, caring, and even human, and discovers great benefits from these interviews: a "limbic resonance" (p. 184), which I assume means something like "good vibes," from these old creatures, a better relationship with her husband, and a good feeling toward her parents. Those old folks just made her feel really better!

Connie Goldman attached a 1992 CD-ROM of the interviewees for our listening at leisure. (Also it is like hearing voices from the grave when Jessica Tandy and some others speak their piece.) In the book, Fay Wray of 1930s King Kong fame says wryly,"90% of the elderly think old age is a tragedy." For that, she is not given any space in the book, only a moment on the disc.

Indeed the purpose of these books is to disprove Ms Wray's observation and there is no problem in finding old people with perky perseverance: they articulate repeatedly "a hang in there, it isn't so bad" message. They proclaim the same theme: that older age people—those past 65—can be happy if they take risks, be creative and be open to change yet keep a connectedness. Then one can find the older years tranquil and enjoyable. It is a matter of either "being aged or ageless" as one says. The book is a self-help manual on how to become an Uber-Elder—or super elder—by living well in old age.

Death is given some space but is treated more of an item on the list of elder issues than a problem or perspective for most of the interviewees. Wisdom, next on the list, is optional and predicated on compassion, simplicity, connectedness and "growing things" (like Cicero's old farmer). All the elder-celebs seem to be pleased to be queried about aging well. Metaphors abound like that of the lobster who must de-shell itself every so often in order to survive. Artie Shaw ends it well with three questions—"Who am I? Where did I come from? Where am I going?" But Artie Shaw leaves his questions unanswered and the book suggests that with age we all answer these questions differently, if at all, and then probably equally well. That makes us in a sense also celebrities.

My problem with "Uber-Elder" celebrity books is that they describe and defend old age rather than define its purpose or role. There is no apparent reason for old age in the society delineated in these books except to find somehow individually a reason for being old and thereby avoiding extinction through suicide. It is a given that the sub-generations have an attitude toward the uselessness of older people, even older Celebs who are mostly forgotten or unknown to them. *Chicken Soup* and *Centenarians* use ordinary people to preach the same message—simplicity, caring, diet, exercise, openness to life's changes will give spiritual and physical succor to the aged and allow an older person to put up with the burden of old age and its purposelessness. Many elderly make up their own roles—caregiver, friend, companion, seeker, advisor and/or provider. Old age can become then a "second act."

These books highlight ironically the valueless-ness of old people in America and western societies. While showing the impact and abilities of the old to make a meaning of their own continued existence, these books emphasize old age's utter unimportance in a productive capitalistic society. Whether they be "secular saints"—celebrities—or just plain folks from the neighborhood, they are expected to tell us why their existence remains important.

They do not expect a "Soylent Green" scenario in which, like the old film, they become part of the food chain; rather, they are expected to enunciate to them-selves and to us <u>why</u> they continue to live as well as <u>how</u>. They all fail because they have no template, no paradigm for purpose. It is every person on his or her own, not only because this is the first time the world has seen so many old people, but because there is yet no defined or accepted reference for these years.

Elders as Prophets

The third segment of contemporary missionaries to the ageing books is "The Prophets." These are the people who propose or reflect an organized philosophy about ageing, usually "it is a special time in the life pattern for you to become a (fill in the blank)."

There is to be sure something reassuring about being told by others that there is a purpose for becoming old, especially if the writer is an authentic elder person.

The Prophets are the social philosophers of ageing—those who give an overall framework to their own older age and suggest the same parameters to their reader. They may use other folks' stories as Cicero did to highlight their own journey and become for us our escort, a modern Sybil to our Aeneas or a Virgil to our Dante But they want us to discover especially the Comedy rather than the Tragedy of ageing. Some of these psycho-pomps are Gail Sheehy, Abigail Trafford, James Hillman, Jimmy Carter, Betty Friedan and Simone de Beauvoir.

These books can give a feeling of confident perseverance to some people. For the ageing Boomers, there is Ram Dass ("Servant of God"), once Richard Alpert and once a guru in the 1970s, but still a disciple of the Indian mystic Baba. Ram Dass shares with us his elder pathways in a personal book entitled *Still Here* (2000). He puts it squarely early on: "older Americans have no mythology to support their presence, no place—figurative or otherwise—in the culture." (p. 25) He presents to us the "common question: Why are we still alive in these useless bodies?" (p. 48) He calls himself "an advance scout for the experiences of aging "(p.204); then he puts us into his perspective to understand the meaning of ageing: a person is a combination of Awareness, Soul and Ego, Ego being that aspect of the self which only "experiences aging and death."(p.29) Life is "the long process of ripening into God" (p. 29) and accomplished by letting the Ego dissolve and the Soul blossom into the Awareness of its true being as part of the eternal Divine. Then we can become—Hooray!—a Buddha ourselves! This personal journey, given meaning by eastern theology, is both an autobiography and a testimony to the value of Ram Dass' life. He has now become a prophet to the ageing since he himself is now old and, sadly, infirmed.

Another prophet is James Hillman who is a popular and scholarly writer. He is a psychologist who offers his own journey model different from that of Dass' but just as meaningful. In *The Force of Character and The Lasting Life* (1999) he argues age discovers and isolates character. Ageing is the anvil of human purpose and is for the individual alone to understand and cherish. It is the period of life that is totally relevant to myself and not to youth or middle age necessities or responsibilities.

Not much comfort here but a steel-eyed spartan recognition of self-value from a popular elder prophet. Hillman writes that time and its brother, age, strip away the frivolous aspects of our personhood and then what is left is character. No humor here, just the plain hard path to self-recognition—and then we get oblivion.

The indomitable Deepak Chopra M.D. would agree. In his *Ageless Body, Timeless Mind* (1993), he argues by embracing an Indian spiritual ayurvedic mind-body framework, we can life longer and age better within a philosophy of acceptance and proper nutrition. B.F. Skinner's *Enjoy Old Age* (reprint, 1997) would add tolerance of one's own failings to Dr. Chopra's list.

But for the generation now undergoing ageing, a familiar name has offered another prophetic map, literally, for growing older: The popular journalist and editor of Vanity Fair magazine, Gail Sheehy.

In *New Passages* (1995), continuing her "passages" brand, she takes us with her through the "flaming fifties" to the "serene sixties." She reports: "I stopped before 50 in *Passages*. Frankly I found it impossible to picture myself at that age. Like so many others of my generation, I could not imagine life beyond 50, and I certainly couldn't bring myself to consider it as a time of special possibility or potential." (p xi) Her book happily combines many stories of confident and unconfident ageing people as examples for the rest of us (e.g., movie actor Cary Grant at 59 refused to kiss the much younger Audrey Hepburn in the film *Charades* [p. 293]) with much popular wisdom—" Exercise appears to be the single most effective non-medical elixir to retard aging.... Long daily walks are part of the job of successful aging." (P.426).

Her proposal for ageing well is to embrace an active ageing rather than a passive ageing. So you can choose how you age. She calls this "sageing"—the process by which men and women accumulate wisdom and grow into the culture's sages."(p.420) She calls a person's 50s "The Age of Mastery" and the 60s, "The

Age of Integrity," it is a "Second Adulthood"—(children gone, house paid, my time—now what?). Not to worry for those who pass the 60s: after 400 plus pages she promises to write next about "the sage seventies and beyond"(p.424). Stay tuned.

Abigail Trafford is also a prophet. Her book is called *My Time* and subtitled "Making the Most of the Bonus Decades after Fifty" (2004). I suggest it should have been entitled JOLTS. Ms Trafford is a columnist for the Washington *Post* and reports her journey into her epiphany: "Little did I know when I started working on this book that it would be my own awakening. Each time I sat down and talked to a person about this stage in life, I got a jolt.... The stories illuminated a richness in human experience that I had never imagined. It was dazzling." (p.255) Her book deals with ages 50 to 80 and is filled with apropos vignettes from people in that age bracket solicited by Ms. Trafford in her attempt to prepare herself and define that generation. She declares "Most people go through a transition period similar to adolescence. (p xxi) She is JOLTED by the time she calls "Second Adolescence" (Part One) since this age shares with teenagers two qualities: Empowerment and Dreaming. (p. 31) Unlike Sheehy, her ageing folks go through a second adolescence, not a second adulthood,—but what's in a name?

"Getting to My Time is the hard part. Once there, you have every chance to flourish. You're not just reinventing a new stage of life for yourself—you're also helping to shape the culture and overturn obsolete barriers against making the most of these bonus decades. You get used to the drumbeat of anxiety." (p 21) JOLT! By the mid fifties, some health problems are likely. (p.25) JOLT! Deaths of colleagues and loved ones occur but "You may find relief after loss." (p.57) Jolt! Perhaps return to school, get a new career, go to a new location—jolt-jolt-jolt! Part Two is called "Seeking Purpose" and tells stories about people in the "creative society" (p.132) they build for themselves and their generation despite adversity or illness. She espouses the idea of "Generactivity" from Erik Erikson—giving back, reaching out, caring for others, helping the community...."(p 107). She finds those who do so leave a legacy to those who follow. JOLT!

Her last section, Nurturing Love (Part Three), delineates friendship, romance and family as meaningful protections against a lonely ageing and an isolated death: "That's one of my goals in MY Time—to go beyond death in order to live."(p.243) Jolt! Her epilogue is called, honest to the gods, "Another Jolt" in which she reconnects with an ex-husband and her stepmother and she goes danc-ing, ending with a breathless—"What's next? I can hardly wait." (p. 259) JOLT! Stay tuned for more of her future jolting "passages."

There is much informal writing in the books by Sheehy and Trafford. They use contractions, eclectic punctuation and short chapters. Also there is a voyeur aspect to both books that may put off an erudite reader seeking for more than Sheehy's and Trafford's unsurprising awakenings.

Is anyone surprised that another prophet is Jimmy Carter? His 2004 book *The Virtues of Aging* could be subtitled "Growing Old with Rosalynn." The former president is a prolific writer with more than a dozen books ranging from a chil-dren's book, *The Little Baby Snoogle-Fleejer* (written with his daughter Amy Carter), to his *Memoirs.* In *Virtues,* one might expect the traditional Christian vir-tues, the classical ones such as Socrates' famous four-justice, moderation, courage, wisdom-or even variations on those two themes.

Rather, like the other prophets, we get an autobiography of his and his wife's experience with ageing thankfully in only 134 pages. After pointing out their problems with becoming suddenly unemployed in 1980 and the financial and current political problems with Social Security (and his advice on how to fix it), he writes about how Rosalynn and he have adapted to each other and to living in Plains, Georgia. He relates that they love their grand children; he tells us what makes up their daily exercise routine; and he illustrates how they stay mentally agile with separate but kitchen connected offices: "Now, well past seventy, Rosa-lynn and I have learned to accommodate each other's desires more accurately and generously, and have never had a more complete and enjoyable relationship." (P.79) Perhaps some readers will think learning that may not be worth the price of the book.

Mr. Carter includes a section on his favorite activities—fishing, hunting, bird-watching, etc.—and prescribes his recipe for "successful aging"—taken from the 1993 MacArthur Foundation report (mentioned above)—Avoid disease and dis-ability, maintain mental and physical health and continue an engagement with life (p.89). Towards the end of this short book he includes a kind of self-selected Elder Hall of Fame—people who are role models for him and perhaps could be for us—his mother, his aunt, his uncle Buddy, his old boss, Admiral Rickover, his Japanese benefactor Rioichi Sasakawa, who gave a major donation to build the Carter Center, and a few more.

Jimmy Carter concludes his study of the virtues of ageing with these instructions: "The simple things—our own happiness, peace, joy, satisfaction, and the exploration of love in all of its forms—are the keys to the virtues of life, at any age." (p. 134.)—All that for only $11.95! Hey, who needs Cicero?

The prophets allow us to pay them a small fee for the book and then have them serve as our escorts or tutors for our journey into ageing. As fellow travelers, we overhear stories about various people—celebrities and ordinary people—who can teach us the same lessons they taught Jimmy, Gail, Abigail, Ram, James, and the rest. The prophets are letting us buy into their own attempt to understand the why and wherefore of their own ageing. They seek reassurance from the aged for themselves and thereby they attempt to become our teachers. As readers, we become thrice removed. Indeed the prophets know how to teach and to entertain, but they do not know how to, or do not want to, define modern old age.

Betty Friedan really did try as she grew older and published her prophetic vision in *The Fountain of Age*. Simone de Beauvoir had published her *Second Sex* in France in 1952; Betty Friedan's *Feminine Mystique* came out in 1963; de Beauvoir's *La Vieillesse* (Old Age) was printed in 1970 (in English 1972) and Friedan's *Fountain of Age* arrived in 1993. While de Beauvoir is scholarly and exhaustive and Friedan suggestive and derivative, I have found them always connected in purpose and pursuit.

Friedan writes to entertain and to persuade. Her *The Feminine Mystique* was a watershed book for its time in the 1960s. She founded various women's movements and encouraged legal abortion, later a national law and still a national controversy.

The 1993 book, also a national best seller, was written for both men and women. In it she is delineating what is by now the usual theme—coping with her ageing by writing a book about her journey. But she was one of the first to do so in America. She is not as scholarly as Simone de Beauvoir who wrote her treatise 23 years earlier, but just as impassioned. She combines statistics about ageing with various selected stories of herself, her friends and many ageing others in 638 pages with much aplomb and even proposes a national solution as an option to deal with the problem of ageing: Euthanasia.

Her book begins seemingly as a women's study guide to growing old: "Because women are, in fact, the great majority of the old, the problems of aging are really women's problems." (p.16). She discovered that most medical studies about ageing were about men, but women live an average of eight years longer then men, to about eighty. So in her 60s, she begins her study of a new feminine issue: ageing.

First she surveys the culture for role models—celebrities, films, advertising, books, television—and finds them all wanting. They offer only stereotyped images, if at all, of the uselessness of being elderly. In most cases the aged are overlooked. She wonders why 65 is the normative year for retirement and finds of course a man was the culprit: The German Chancellor Otto von Bismarck. (He chose 65 because he found the suicide rate higher for men after 65 in the late nineteenth century than for women.) Friedan believes America now has forced retirement. Old age in America is seen to be a "problem" and therefore it should be open to solutions; but the problem is not given any solutions since it is a part of life peculiarly neither respected nor deemed important. It is only to be endured. Well, says Betty, we'll see about that and she begins to offer some solutions.

After examining the usual losses of ageing—sexual, psychological, economic, social—through relevant vignettes and national data, she soldiers on with the section called "New Choices": Older age should be a time for change, growth and adventure. Her book is an elder anthology of usually upbeat stories of senior citizens coping well in adversity, illness, and turmoil who become mentors for her. Many indeed seem to be thriving in older age. She eschews the youth culture as an irrelevant hoax and sees nursing homes as concentration camps for the elderly, the alien "them." But, finally, and after many examples, she accepts herself as one of "them."

Her last section is entitled "Transcendence: The Freedom to Risk" and argues for "adventurous aging": "an active creation or recreation of those ties that are as essential to our humaneness as food and water to our physical existence...." (p 583). She suggests these adventures could be learning and doing new things at Elderhostels, the University of the Third Age, Senior Centers, the local college, etc. Then there is a commitment to social engagement, family reconnecting, community action, and, under the same rubric we saw earlier in Trafford's book, an espousal of good old Eric Erikson's "Generactivity" which is also the title of her last chapter—and finally also her mantra.

After many stimulating pages, the best we get from her is her prophetic epiphany—if not redemption: "I recognized my own compelling need to transcend the war between the sexes…I recognized my need to reconcile feminism and families comes from my own generactivity, my personal truth as mother to my children, and my commitment to the future through the women's movement. The unexpectedness of this new quest has been my adventure into age…. I never have felt so free." (p.638) The book is worth reading for the stories she tells of others grappling and often achieving positive ageing but it is not to be read for her self-congratulatory conclusion. There is not that much fresh water in her Fountain.

Simone de Beauvoir's redoubtable 1970 study called *La Vieillesse* (in English, *The Coming of Age*) is the best book on the subject since Cicero. It has historic depth, majestic erudition, embedded cleverness (Part Two is called "Being-in-the-World," a pun derived from her long time lover Jean Paul Sartre's philosophical principle of "En-Soi") and a good old-fashioned French leftist political vision. I especially like it for its demand on the reader to pay attention, something most modern books do not require. Simone does not want to entertain, but to engage us and argue with us.

Simone de Beauvoir when approaching her old age did what every good French scholar does: She researched the history, biology, ethnology, literature and mythology of old age. She produced in 1970 an anthology of international and historical elder information and, though now sometimes dated, it still the most in depth presentation about human ageing extent. She proudly entitled it *La Vieillesse* ("Old Age"). Combining her abilities as a scholar and a writer with her socialist anger, she embroils us in a nearly 600 page treatise which is still readable and interesting.

"The fact that for the last fifteen or twenty years of his life a man should be no more than a reject…reveals the failure of our civilization…. Insisting that men should remain men during the last years of their life would imply a total upheaval of our society…. I call upon my readers to help me in doing so." (pp. 6-7)

She characterizes the many traits of old age as being also its possible opportunities: Selective memory, limited interests, ambition, refocus of passions, fear and suspicion, security of habit, emotionalism, interest in legacy (e.g. grandchildren), "senile delinquency" (antisocial behavior caused by one's feeling of social exclusion), the liberation to act and the balm of projects yet to undertake. Indeed various mental and physical illnesses, lack of curiosity, senile dementia, poor care, weakness of character, financial misfortune and just bad luck may limit or nullify those opportunities for fully participating in the possible benefits of ageing.

She argues that while there is no satisfactory social role for the old in western society; however, some older individuals have influenced their times with independence and energy. She exemplifies her points about agile ageing with many selected biographies: Voltaire, Victor Hugo, Michelangelo, Verdi, Lou Andreas-Salome, Freud, Chateaubriand, Lamartine, Tolstoy, Whitman, Casanova and others. They infiltrate her book and become mentors for her; they allow her to visualize a generally successful elder life for herself despite the anxieties and adversities of her ageing.

But they are only individual stories and perhaps only useful models for her. Society's position (except in China and some other socialist nations) she maintains remains unchanged: The old are useless and decaying appendages to a progressive society.

She makes sure we understand her commitment: "There is only one solution if old age is not to be an absurd parody of our former life, and that is to go on pursuing ends that give our existence a meaning—devotion to individuals [she had Sartre], to groups or to causes [she had socialism], social, political, intellectual or creative work [her book].... One's life has value so long as one attributes value to the life of others, by means of love, friendship, indignation, compassion....It is far better not to think about it too much, but to live a fairly committed, fairly justified life so that one may go on in the same path even when all illusions have vanished and one's zeal for life has died away." (pp. 540-41) That is all there is.

It is society's fault that there is neither role nor purpose for being old. Yes, individuals like Voltaire and Hugo can influence society and enjoy productive and remarkable old ages, but in general society degrades or renders invisible old age and, because of meager social benefits, the younger generations have neither current guilt nor future awareness. The aged are aliens who are to be stored and forgotten in a bourgeois world. "It is the whole system that is at issue and our claim cannot be otherwise than radical—change life itself." (p. 543) However, her changes would comfort few people but her.

Simone would not go gentle into her old age. She is in my view the best read and most challenging of the prophets, but as the rest, limited by her own ageing auto-biographical needs. She and the rest want to be elder saviors but cannot construct and impart a comprehensive creed.

The Minor Prophets

There are four other "Prophet" subspecies which should be mentioned: One I will label "Whole Life Pilgrimage" books (not only dealing with old age or elder issues) such as the autobiographical two-story mountain *Nearer My God* (1996) by William F. Buckley, Jr. or the charming *L'Art d'Etre un Grand Pere* by Victor Hugo (1877); witty, chatty, often dated "Elder Memoirs" such as *Over 50…So What!* (1961) by the late chanteuse, Hildegarde (Loretta Sell), and that of the spunky Phyllis Diller called *The Joys of Aging and How to Avoid Them* (1981) (out of print); thirdly, the "Elder Poets," who offer us humor or philosophy as strate-gies against old age: There is the lame "book for obsolete children" called *You're Only Old Once* (1986) by Dr. Seuss (Theodore Geisel), *Suddenly Sixty* (2000), a collection of a few whimsical, insightful poems (e.g.,"1963-Niagra//1999-Via-gra") by Judith Viorst (which reminds me of Christopher Matthew's *Now We Are Sixty* (1999)—which is to remind one of A.A. Milne's book for six year olds, *Now We are Six*—and includes some cute ditties such as "Life": "When I was One/ …The War had begun//When I was Fifty/I turned very thrifty//But now that I'm Sixty, I've got to confess/That more often than not, I couldn't care less"), Ogden Nash's delightful *I Wouldn't Have Missed It: Selected Poems* (1975) (out of print), the iconic W.B. Yeats who in his late sixties wrote "A Dialogue of Self and Soul"(1929-1933), suggesting reincarnation as an anodyne to old age:

> So great a sweetness flows into the breast
> We must laugh and we must sing,
> We are blest by every thing,
> Every thing we look upon is blest.

and so he urged us to persevere and prevail in late life in "A Prayer for Old Age" (1934-1935):

> I pray…
> That I may seem, though I die old,
> A foolish, passionate man.

And, similarly, a half-century earlier, the enthusiastic Walt Whitman in "Youth, Day, Old Age and Night," included in his *Leaves of Grass* (1881), welcomed later life as a timely blessing:

> Youth, large, lusty, loving—youth full of grace, force, fascination-
> Do you know that Old Age may come after you with equal grace, force, fascination?
> Day full-blown and splendid—day of the immense sun, action, ambition, laughter-
> The night follows close with millions of suns, and sleep and restoring darkness.

The last, the fourth "Prophet" sub-specie, I call the "Grief and Death" writers, such as the mother text for a religious death, *Ars Moriendi* (The Art of Dying) (1589), the modern *How We Die* (1995) by Dr. Sherwin B. Nuland (who noted it is illegal to die in America except by disease), and the ultimate "how to do it to yourself" book by Derek Humphrey, *Final Exit*, which is about suicide ("save those pills") and published by the Hemlock Society in 1994.

A fifth sub-species could be the "After Life" or "Death and Dying" authors such as the late Elizabeth Kubler-Ross M.D. who authored eighteen books on the subject (e.g., *On Death and Dying* [1969] and *On Life After Death* [1991]) or Carol Zaleski's *Otherworld Journeys: Accounts of Near Death Experience in Medieval and Modern Times* (1987). But I do not include them because that topic is different from how to live an artful old age and is grounds for another eclectic essay. Those ladies join Homer, Plato, Virgil, Dante, T.S. Eliot and currently Mitch Albom as our escorts to explore the myths and experiences of the after-life journey, still understandably a compelling topic after three millennia of narratives.

One can find these books in larger bookstores, usually placed in the section that also offers texts on retirement planning, grief and grieving and death and dying. So much for Solon and Erickson!

The central problem we all now face is that in former centuries, there was a need for the elderly to pass on their farming and household skills to their progeny; but there is no need now for old people with dated skills in a constantly changing technological society. There is a song, sung by very young people in an old play written by Leonard Bernstein called *West Side Story* and entitled: "There's a place for us, somewhere a place for us...." The elderly remember it well and feel its sting.

Sigmund Freud said all men need work and love. We have Viagra, Levitra and other medicinal aids for the elderly for the latter, but society still has not grappled with elder work that signifies worth and purpose. A major, growing segment of humanity, the old, has but one characteristic—living longer than needed in a capitalistic society and thereby legally rendered at 65 officially useless and individually purposeless. But that will change drastically and quickly.

It is unlikely the United States will ever behave like many African, Latin American, Asian and Islamic cultures that honor the aged as social resources for which the family is ultimately responsible. But the 21st century will become the world's first "Silver Century" because there will be more people over 60 than under15. Then America may change in some ways since it will become important to find meaningful roles for a vast number of ageing Americans.

Perhaps this large block of older citizens will: form a political party emulating Israel's "Power to the Pensioners" to ensure their interests; dedicate a national holiday to the elderly such as the one in Japan called "Respect the Aged Day"; increase taxes as in Sweden and Finland to afford model home care and support services for older citizens; extend the retirement age to 75 and form, as in Japan, Elder Employment Centers for qualified 65-80 year old people; recognize volunteer activity from homecare to public services as socially legitimate work for older citizens; spend more on geriatric and gerontology research and medical services; with the predicted flood of centenarians, legislate 85 as the start of official old age; add "Ageism" to "Racism" on the list of American political taboos; and include a segment on ageing within the formal high school education curriculum of the rising generation, the "Millennials" or "Echo Boomers" (1982-2002).

Before her death in October of 2003 at age 116, Kamato Hongo, then the oldest living person in the world, was asked by the Japanese press her recipe for longevity. She told them: "Not to worry too much." The longevity crown was passed to a Dutch lady who died in 2005 at 115, Hendrikje van Andel-Schipper. She reportedly told interested reporters her own prescription for attaining old age: "a herring a day and a glass of orange juice for the vitamins." Now the oldest living person, also a woman, is an American named Elisabeth Borden who was born on 15 August 1890. So far she has wisely given no sound bytes to the media when asked about her remarkable age, but perhaps if she did, she might quote Shakespeare:

WITH MIRTH AND LAUGHTER, LET OLD WRINKLES COME.

To conclude this cultural and literary digest of books about ageing, I quote from Paul Theroux's voyager testament from his *Dark Star Safari* (2003): "What all older people know, what had taken me almost sixty years to learn, is that an aged face is misleading. I did not want to be the classic bore, the reminiscing geezer, yet I now knew: the old are not as frail as you think, and they are insulted to be regarded as feeble. They are full of ideas, hidden powers, even sexual energy. Don't be fooled by the thin hair and battered features and skepticism. The older traveler knows it best: in our hearts we are youthful, and we are insulted to be treated as old men and burdens, for we have come to know that the years have made us more powerful and streetwise. Years are not an affliction. Old age is strength." (p.198)

Cicero would agree enthusiastically.

Despite so much help from the Bible, the ancients, history, Merchants, Mentors and Prophets, millions of us will have to define our old age for ourselves as we grow into it.

I wish you, my fellow traveler, a Bon Voyage.

—Peter Abbey

CHAPTER ONE

GUIDANCE

You must remember this,
A kiss is just a kiss,
A sigh is just a sigh;
The fundamental things apply,
As time goes by.

As Time Goes By, by Herman Hupfield (1931)

AGEING:
THE CHRISTIAN
PERSPECTIVE

Cicero (106–43BC) is the literary and philosophical arbiter of judgments made about ageing and old age in the classical era. And although he wrote his essay on that subject before the Christian era, his insights are provocative and sound astoundingly contemporary. He encourages his readers not only to accept the inevitable chronological stage of old age, but to rejoice in it, for it is the crowning moment of human life, the best time of anyone's existence. He wrote "On Old Age" with a practical objective in mind, that is to provide comfort and solace to those who fear the uncertainties of old age:

> My dear Laelius and Scipio, we must stand up against old age and make up for its drawbacks by taking pains. We must fight it as we should an illness. We must look after our health, use moderate exercise, take just enough food and drink to recover, but not to overload, our strength. Nor is it the body alone that must be supported, but the intellect and soul much more. For they are like lamps, unless you feed them with oil, they too go out from old age…The fact is that old age is respectable just as long as it asserts itself, maintains its proper rights, and is not enslaved to anyone. For as I admire a young man who has something of the old man in him, so do I an old one who has something of a young man. The man who aims at this may possibly become old in body—in mind he never will. [1]

It is Cicero's intention to counter the dour arguments and complaints of the older citizens of Rome, who believed that old age is the occasion for unhappiness. He postulated that there are four reasons for complaints about old age:

> The fact is that when I come to think it over, I find that there are four reasons for old age being thought unhappy: First, that withdraws us from active employments: second, that it enfeebles the body; third, that it deprives us of nearly all physical pleasures; fourth, that it is the next step to death. Of each of these reasons, if you will allow me, let us examine the force and justice separately. [2]

Cicero proceeds slowly and logically to counter all four arguments.

First, he argues that the active employment of physical activity of youth cannot and should not be the important activity of old age, rather in old age, the faculty of the intellect becomes dominant an one can be active all the day long in acts of adv ice and consent to those in positions of political power.

Second, "although bodily strength is wanting in old age", bodily strength is not demanded from old men. Old men are not required to perform duties which require vigorous physical powers.

Third, that old age reduces the necessity of sensual pleasures is not a hardship but a great blessing: "What a splendid service does old age render, if it takes from us the greatest blot of youth"! Sensual pleasure is a "deadly curse" inflicted upon mankind by nature. When we are old we are no longer afflicted by this youthful wanton quality. Most of the tragedies of early life are caused by the prurient urges of youth: "treasons, revolutions, (and) secret communications with the enemy". Sensual pleasures lead us all in our youth to crime, evil deeds, fornications and adulteries, which all work against the intellectual integrity of the human being.

Fourth, the fear of death is truly not an event to be feared, and most people who use their intellects discover early on that "death is not a think to be feared". Cicero believed that the soul was immortal, though he never postulated such a theological belief as a certifiable fact. How could anyone possibly do that?

> It is by these means, my dear Scipio—for you and Laelius were wont to express surprise on this point,—that my old age sits lightly on me, and is not only not oppressive but even delightful. But if I am wrong in thinking the human soul immortal, I am glad to be wrong; nor will I allow the mistake which gives me so much pleasure to be wrested from me as long as I live. But if when dead, as some insignificant philosophers think, I am to be without sensation, I am not afraid of dead philosophers deriding my errors. Again, if we are not to be immortal, it is nevertheless what a man must wish—to have his life end at its proper time. For nature puts a limit to living as to everything else. Now, old age is as it were the playing out of the drama, the full fatigue of which we should shun, especially when we also feel that we have had more than enough of it. [3]

Cicero is fundamentally a Stoic, a convincing philosophical position, which affirms the priority of mind over matter, the spirit over the flesh. It is a philosophical and spiritual position which has won many adherents both in the Classical Greek and Roman worlds and later, in tangential ways, in the Renaissance and also in the modern world. Desiderius Erasmus used many Stoic ideas in his theological perspective, which was at odds with one kind of Reformation "Orthodoxy" but which, for Erasmus, enhanced his understanding of the Christian faith.

Another example was the Italian Pico della Mirandola, who also seems to be a happy union of Stoicism and Christian Platonism.

The above is my introduction to my essay "On Ageing: A Christian Perspective". I do want to acknowledge the strong influence of Stoicism on the thinking of the Early Christian Church, but I want to argue in this essay that Christianity and Stoicism, though similar in their concepts, ultimately are different perspectives of the world. And the remainder of this essay will attempt to say why.

What follows is my perspective of the Christian faith and its relation to Old Age. I want to affirm three Christian theological points which, I believe, are essential to a sound and realistic judgment about Old Age. Of course, I encourage other Christians to say it differently.

First is an acute sense of one's own mortality. Cicero affirms the same principle, but attempts to place the morbid and tragic experiences of life apart from our consciousness. The Christian wants to make it central to any awareness of old age. The Existentialists have pointed out that Christian theology from Saint Paul to Jean Calvin has been written in the consciousness of death. For the clearly articulated knowledge about death *unveils* the deepest and most realistic possibilities of life.

My teacher Carl Michalson has tutored me in much of what I am now affirming. Michalson tells the story of Philip of Macedon, in the pre-Christian world, that he employed a slave to enter his sleeping quarters every morning to announce, and to shout at the top of his voice, "Philip, remember that thou too must die".[4]

Now I do not w ant to portray the role of one's mortality as some kind of mortuary drama. Christians have done that, much to their personal distress—there is sufficient news of death and its imminence in the daily news reports. However, to acknowledge that we are mortal (God is immortal, therefore, by a simple logical move, humans cannot be) rather than making us psychologically morbid and maudlin, actually allows us to examine every day's human experiences. We can then affirm that the life lived by *memento mori* anticipates one's actual death and allows all of the fears and anxieties attendant upon one's death to be overcome.

If death is a fact of one's own history, that fact, intellectually at least, ought not to create an intellectual crisis. A psychological or spiritual one can be mitigated by the Christian affirmation that, though we shall surely die, we are not dead yet. A psychological reaction takes place by which we may focus our hopes and aspirations on the events and experiences of every single day. We carry the sentence of death within us, as Saint Paul affirmed, so that we will not trust totally in ourselves. (2 Cor 1:9).

The fourteenth century artist Hans Holbein carved a series of figures which he called "The Dance of Death". Everyone is included, from every station of life, from king to peasant, cardinal to priest, grandparent to infant. Death is not respecter of persons: "Philip, remember that thou too must die".

No one can take another's place in death. No one can die your death for you. This knowledge heightens our sense of one's own irreplaceability and heightens one's self-consciousness. We are aware of our essential nature that is of a mortal human being distinct from all other human beings, except for the fact of our own biological death. But it is my death; my death inspires the sense of the utter uniqueness of every person's life. In the presence of death, everyone is different.

Samuel Johnson said that a "life worthy of rational being must be always in progressions. We must purpose to do better than in the past." That is an accurate way of looking at the Christian life. There are limits to our lives, we do not know what they are, but we are alive now and we can take full advantage of all of the capacities and abilities given to us—day by day.

We are reminded of the prayer of Jan Austen, *circa* 1811,

> Teach us…that we may feel the importance
> of every day, of every hour, as it passes.

Second is the acceptance of human suffering. At this point, we shall sever any philosophical connection with Cicero's Stoicism. Suffering is a harsh and real fact of human life. It is not illusory, it is not soul-edifying nor does it provide an easy solution to "Why should good people suffer?" It may not be overcome by positive thoughts or good sentiments. Suffering is the experience of pain, sickness, loneliness, anxiety, misfortune, psychological ailments, and finally, the experience of the death of a loved one. "Why did this happen to me?—" is the revelatory cry of someone suffering who does not know the reason why. It seems that it is only the human being who can ask the question "Why?" as one senses an affliction for which he lacks an answer.

The notable Soren Kierkegaard in 19th Century Denmark saw suffering not as incidental to life, but as instrumental to it. That is why he said that there can be joy in suffering; it is not an accidental condition of life, it is rather a fundamental part of life itself, it is part and parcel of the process of life itself. It is too assuring a statement to say, as Soren Kierkegaard did "that the way of suffering is the right way." It is for me not at all the right way—a life without suffering is highly desirable—but it is not the true way, it is not the real way. As the apostle Paul wrote of suffering: "My grace is sufficient for you, for my power is made perfect in weakness." I will all the more gladly boast of my weaknesses, that the power of Christ may rest upon me. For the sake of Christ, then, I am content with weaknesses, insults, hardships, persecutions, and calamities: for when I am weak, then I am strong." (2 Cor. 12:9,10). (cf. Romans 817; 2 Peter 2: 20ff.; Acts 9:16; Phil. 1:29.)

Suffering is not a character-builder, but is a prescribed feature of every life, a *given*, a datum of human existence, with which every human being must wrestle. Dietrich Bonhoeffer, the Christian martyr during World War II knew this fact very well when he reported in *Prisoner for God* that "It is the divine revelation to a suffering world that in the world there will be suffering, even unto God himself." And, of course, this is the decisive difference between Christianity and all of the other religions of the world.

The Bible directs the Christian to the suffering servant who is not merely the paradigm for all suffering, but is also the agent of God whose divine purpose is to give some reason for the experience of suffering. Suffering is, as one might say, a normative human experience. But Christians are convinced that because of the suffering of Christ on the Cross, there is some ultimate meaning to it all, and perhaps only an eschatological explanation may make ultimate sense. I know of philosophers and theologians who have spent long lives in search of an answer to the problem of suffering, only to admit that there may not be one after all.

What helps me, both intellectually and personally, is to affirm that I know that God does not intend our suffering:

> Will the mystery break itself open and reveal the intention which lies behind the suffering? If we could know that and if we could justify it, we could accept the suffering without crisis. In the Christian faith that cur-

tain is lifted and this mystery is unveiled: *we can know that God does not intend our suffering.*[5]

To know that our suffering is not in God's purpose suggests some way to find the emotional and spiritual (even may I warrant, intellectual) grounds for equanimity in suffering:

> To know, not that God creates the evil but hates it, to know that it rises up against him as it does against us, to know that it will yield, if it yield at all, not to a gesture of omnipotence but to the steady persistence of suffering love.[6]

Third is a realistic hope of eternal life. Cicero argues (with Ennius, his contemporary) "that death is not a subject for mourning when it is followed by immortality."

> For I do not see why I should not venture to tell you my personal opinion as to death, of which I seem to myself to have a clearer vision in proportion as I am nearer to it. I believe, Scipio and Laelius, that your fathers—those illustrious men and my dearest friends—are still alive, and that too with a life which alone deserves the name. For as long as we are imprisoned in this framework of the body, we perform a certain function and laborious work assigned to us by fate. The soul, in fact, is of heavenly origin, forced down from its home in the highest, and, so to speak, buried in earth, a place quite opposed to its divine nature and its immortality.[7]

The soul is freed from the laborious imprisonment of the body, the soul, in fact, is of heavenly origin:

> Oh glorious day when I shall set out to join that heavenly conclave and company of souls, and depart from the turmoil and impurities oft this world: For I shall not go to join only those whom I have before mentioned, but also my son Cato, than whom no better man was ever born, nor one more conspicuous for piety.[8]

But Cicero goes on to argue that he is not certain about the immortality of the soul, and that life ends "at its proper time."

Here we see the classic expression of the doctrine of the immortality of the soul, the immortal soul is imprisoned within a mortal body. The same argument is found in Plato's *Apology* and *The Phaedo*. With the death of the person, the soul which has been attempting for all of life to escape from the body, finally succeeds. And the soul then is united heavenward with the Absolute Soul, the Divine Intelligence, the Platonic Forms, the Heavenly Ideas, etc.

The Christian affirmation of the resurrection of the dead, which is the single most positive belief of Christians, that we who love Jesus will rise from the dead just like Jesus. The founder of an ancient religion, a great moral teacher, someone who introduced into the whole world a new spirituality, for all of his human accomplishments, is led to a dratted cross, there to die, not indiscriminately, nor accidentally, but to die for you and me, and to provide for us the way to eternal life. William James, the great Harvard psychologist and philosopher, said that most religious people believe because of the promise of life after death.

The sense of the universality of death inspires the sense of the utter uniqueness of every person's life. "This one will never live again," is more than a homiletical warning, it is a primary fact of all of our lives. And the Christian confidence in life after death offers an antidote to the most morbid and ghoulish of fears.

The geography of heaven remains a mystery, but we can affirm with Christians for the last 2000 years, with a sure and certain confidence, that it is a world of light and peace. As St. Paul proclaims in 1 Corinthians 15: 51-57,

> Lo! I tell you a mystery. We shall not all sleep, but we shall all be changed, in a moment, in the twinkling of an eye, at the last trumpet. For the trumpet will sound, and the dead will be raised imperishable, and we shall be changed. For this perishable nature must put on the imperishable, and this mortal nature must put on immortality. When the perishable puts on the imperishable, and the mortal puts on immortality, then shall come to pass the saying that is written: "Death is swallowed up in victory."

We open all the stops, and can sing of

> The strife is oer the battle done
> The victory of life is won
> The song of triumph has begun
> ALLELUIA

Now the laborer's task is over
Now the battle day is past
Now upon the farther shore
Lands the voyager at last
Father in thy gracious keeping
Leave we now that servant sleeping

The Christian has some knowledge of who God is from his scrutiny of the Biblical record. God is the Being who is "from everlasting to everlasting" and that His revelation in Jesus Christ is both "the beginning and the end". So we may be assured that the sufferings of all human beings are *not* in the willful intention of God. "We shall all be changed", our lives will ultimately (again the notion of eschatologically seems appropriate) be conformed to the divine intent. Our bad days are numbered, (cf. 2 Cor. 4:17), it will not last forever. And it seems clear to me that you can stand almost anything if you know that it will not last forever. God has revealed His purpose for His creation—it is a covenant of love with all of humanity. It is the Christian's conviction that God has arranged through His Son to establish at the end of time, and at the end of our lives, what He purposed in the beginning, that is, a world that is good—with human beings who no longer experience the ravages of suffering.

—William A. Johnson

Footnotes

1. Cicero, "On Old Age" (*De Senectute*): *Greek and Roman Classics in Translation,* eds. Charles Theophilus Murphy, Kevin Guinagh, Whitney Jennings Oates, Longmans, Green and Co., 1955, (p. 826)

2. Cicero, "On Old Age", *op. cit*, (p.820)

3. *Op cit,* (p.840)

4. Carl Michalson, *Faith for Personal Crises,* Charles Scribner's Sons,1958, (p.160f.)

5. Carl Michalson, *op. cit,* (p.152)

6. Edwin Lewis, *The Creator and the Adversary,* (p.21)

7. Cicero, *op. cit.,* (p.837)

8. Cicero, *op. cit.,* (p.839)

THE BUDDHIST WAY
OF
AGEING

Buddhism Falls into two major sects, the basic tenets are the same except that the Hinayana sect (India and Southeast Asia) does not accept Buddha as a deity; the Mahayana sect (China, Japan, Tibet and the Mongolias) feels that he is. Being a Hinayana Buddhist, I do not believe in a deity or the Eastern concept of an after-life. Impermanence was considered by Cicero (*On Old Age, Bks. VII-VIII*), but he preferred immortality. I present another view for those concerned with old age but who find the Western concepts of immortality difficult to accept.

OLD AGE, DEATH AND DYING

The concerns with old age and death are universal and the Buddha's focus was primarily on these issues 2500 years ago. He became obsessed by the suffering of sickness, old age and death which had been hidden from him in his you by his overprotective family and they came as a shock to him when he was suddenly and accidentally exposed to them. So much so, that he left his family and became a monk hoping to find the answer to suffering in his religion (he was born a Hindu). After years of trying one Hindu discipline after another, he abandoned them all for lack of success. However, he had discovered the first of his eight NOBLE TRUTHS (as they are called):

SUFFERING IS UNIVERSAL

Years passed trying to understand what was the cause of suffering. One day under a Bodh tree, he realized the answer—the second NOBLE TRUTH:

THE CAUSE OF SUFFERING IS DESIRE.

The third NOBLE TRUTH followed:

DESIRE MUST BE OVERCOMED

And the fourth NOBLE TRUTH is:

DESIRE CAN BE OVERCOME BY MODERATION AND FOLLOWING THE EIGHT FOLD PATH.

It was these discoveries that made him the Enlightened One or "The Buddha." These Four Noble Truths seem so simplistic at face value that I had a hard time accepting them as anything profound. I struggled with the second Noble Truth for years. How could all pain and suffering be reduced to desire? But over the years, I continued to ask: Is this particular pain and suffering caused by desire? And, I came to realize that yes, desire played a key role in creating and intensifying all pain and suffering. I am not taking about a toothache or stubbing one's toe, but the pain and suffering in seeing a loved one age and die, of people struggling with fatal diseases and other hopeless conditions where dying was painful and for me, heart wrenching. And always, it was my deep desire to prevent their suffering and dying that caused the greatest pain and suffering within me.

Later, when I was to experience my own personal pain and sicknesses and potentially fatal conditions, again, it was my desire to be free of them that caused me more suffering than the actual conditions themselves. Here, the Buddha's teachings were my greatest source of strength and comfort. For the Buddha taught that desire must (and can) be overcome. And here one perceives the true greatness of the Buddha. It is only with acceptance of the nature of life, of the universality of pain and suffering, old age, death and dying that we free ourselves of hopeless desires. I learned that there would be no definition of life if it were eternal and that death is inherent within the concept of life. We are born, live and die—a continuum that we must accept or suffer hopeless desires in trying to deny it.

THE PARABLE OF THE MUSTARD SEED

There is the famous parable in which a child has died. The mother is heartbroken. She cannot stand her pain and goes to the Buddha and begs him to restore life to her child. He tells her: If I am to restore life to your child I need the mustard seed from a home where no child has previously died. She rushes off to obtain the mustard seed. However, in each house she inquires, she is told that, alas, a child has died there at one time or another. After trying endlessly and without success to find a house where no child has died, she returns to the Buddha and says: "I realize what you were trying to tell me: my suffering is the same as every other mother whose child has died and that my desire to bring back my child is the same as every other distressed mother; but, if I finally accept my loss, as they have, it will be easier to bear."

THE EIGHT FOLD PATH

(Right Understanding, Right Thought, Right Speech, Right Action, Right Livelihood, Right Effort, Right Mindfulness and Right Concentration.)

As often as I try, I can never remember each one of the Eight Fold Path the Buddha taught for overcoming personal desire. In essence they are: Moderation, right thought and intentions, right endeavors, right living and action, and right deeds. In fact, the four Noble Truths and the Eight Fold Path are the entire Bible of Buddhism, the rest is merely expounding on these principles along with parables and discourses to further clarify their meaning. There are no "Thou Shalt Nots" laws or other constraints. The onus is on the individual to explore within oneself how to overcome desire through the Eight Fold Path. For example: How does one teach oneself acceptance of dying through right thinking. This is a lifelong analysis of one's self and how to look beyond the present, beyond the self, to the universal. Perhaps the best English exposition of these concepts is Herman Hesses's "Siddhartha" (which is the first name of Siddartha Gotama, the man who became The Enlightened One or "The Buddha").

HAPPINESS

The present Dalai Lama (a Mahayana Buddhist) whom I have met several times at our temple has said: "The purpose of life is Happiness." While I am not a Mahayana Buddhist, I agree completely. (Both sects of Buddhism are like family and have never to my knowledge had the religious wars seen in Christianity or Islam). Again, how can one find Happiness as a goal in life? The Eight fold Path gives the blueprint but not the actual details because as the Buddha said "no one can teach another their religion (or path) for they have to find it for themselves." That is why we have no baptism, no sins, no formal structure to guide us. Our own introspection of our thoughts and deeds should help us find the way to true happiness—not the fun of getting a new car, or expensive toys, but an inner happiness that sustains us in this transient existence.

REINCARNATION AND NIRVANA

Both Reincarnation and Nirvana are Hindu concepts that predate the Buddha by thousands of years and are baggage that he inherited. They were and are concepts that still pervade both Hinduism and Buddhism. What then is Reincarnation and Nirvana?

REINCARNATION

Simply put, reincarnation is the "rebirth into another individual or living being after death." As it came from Hinduism, it tried to explain what happens to those unresolved desires and negative thoughts that were not resolved prior to death. This "energy" (called Karma) presumable passes on to another life form when one dies. It is not a conscious "transfer" and is essentially only a metaphysical concept. Some find solace in such a concept. I personally do not.

But, what does this concept mean to me as an American and as a Buddhist? Reincarnation is not something one can deal with as it seems to me too speculative. If we have no awareness of a future life then why philosophize about one? We would not want to pass bad genes on to any future generations and, if there is a Karma, we would naturally not want to pass that on either. We can avoid it through the Eight Fold path which we follow for more reasons that just Karma. In any event, I do not find it an important issue.

NIRVANA

Buddhism does not preach an afterlife in the Western sense, that is, a life after death where one meets friends and relatives in the presence of a deity. That to us is the result of a desire to deny death and frustrates the acceptance of our true transient existence.

Nirvana is called a "state of bliss" that one achieves when one dies and all Karma has been resolved. Again, there is no conscious transfer of the individual to this state. It is a return to the oneness with the universe from which we came. Cremation is symbolic of the dispersion of the individual to nothingness which is translated as "oneness with the universe" with nothing of the "individual" remaining.

Nirvana is more complex than one might conjecture. I am a retired physician, a neurophysiologist and scientist. "Bliss" is an emotion and emotions are perceived through the complexity of the Limbic system in the brain. Once the brain is dead, there are no emotions, no bliss in the scientific sense. However, the issue of consciousness cannot be as easily dismissed when one contemplates Nirvana.

I evolved a theory in 1983 when lecturing at the University of Charleston based on evolution and Buddhism. Basically I stated that what we call consciousness or awareness should not be reserved for only "human consciousness" as many scientists do. They even deny consciousness to other animals such as dogs or cats, let alone to ants and other minute creatures. Yet, these creatures respond in identical ways to ourselves in similar situations of seeking food and avoiding danger. Therefore, is consciousness or awareness pervasive in all forms of life? I would have to say "Yes." But where then does it originate? If other attributes evolve, awareness must evolve too, but from what? While most scientists would agree that no organ springs from nothing ("*de novo*"), they readily agree that basic consciousness or awareness did.

If consciousness, or more simply "awareness", is a universal trait of all living things, is it then not an inherent property of all matter and energy in an even simpler form? As a scientist and a Buddhist I have to accept that it is a universal trait of all matter and energy which is too primitive or subtle to discern. And is it this subtle awareness that responds to new situations by organizing a reaction.

Buddhism preaches a continuity of everything and an interrelatedness of all things which is both rational and scientifically sound as we are coming to realize. We are in a continuum and merely changing states from one form to another. The one constant in the universe is Change. One does not have to study neurophysiology to see how an external stimulus affects an organism, which then affect the very cells of the organism, which in turn affect the internal physiology of the cell and eventually the nucleus and DNA of those cells. The result is change. The change may be small or large, brief or permanent. There is no magic, no deity, no survival of the fittest. It is pure physiology. Today, we have the means of studying it in the most finite detail each step of the way. And we can see the cause of effect, each step of the way.

But why go into this digression when discussing Nirvana? It may seem obvious to you by now that I believe while "human consciousness" dies when the brain dies, the more primitive and pervasive awareness that is inherent in matter and energy persists forever. So the symbolic cremation to destroy the body and return the atoms and energy back to their original basic state of awareness is not an unreasonable concept. What is hard to accept is the concept that such a primitive awareness is bliss. For all practical purposes it is beyond our comprehension to grasp such a state of awareness and to know if such a state is bliss or otherwise. In any event, Nirvana supports the concept of the continuity of our place in the universe where we are now and will always belong.

LONELINESS

There is a parable in Buddhism which I often remember when people ask me if I fear being alone when I am dying. The parable deals with a man who sees his aged mother going somewhere on a road that is very icy and slippery and she is having a hard time holding her balance. He goes to her and says: "Let me help you, it is so dangerous on this ice and you are all alone." She replies: "I came into this world alone and I will go out of this world alone. No one can accompany me on either journey. So I am not afraid to be alone on this journey." She continued by herself slipping and sliding on her way into the distance as her son watches her go.

When one contemplates one's life, its briefness, the pain and suffering that we strive to overcome, we begin to realize that we are dealing with these emotions within ourselves and no one can accompany us there. In this sense, we are truly alone. However, when one has a rich inner life, one learns to enjoy the happiness of this transient existence. When we learn that everyone is traveling in the same direction by different roads to the same oneness with the universe, there is a sense of camaraderie and peace. In this sense, we are not alone.

Friedrich Nietzche said in "Man and Superman" that the superman is the one who stands alone on the mountain top, a leader, who, in taking on the responsibility of those below, breathes a cooler and fresher air than others. In Buddhism, we are alone in the sense that perceiving the universal frees us from the immediate and the personal. One learns to accept this loneliness as one accepts our transient existence.

INTROSPECTION VS MATERIALISM

Introspection is a large part of Buddhism in order to find the right path, the right actions, the right attitude and the right deeds. It requires solitude and time to think especially if we are to find the acceptance of life as it is, not as we would want it to be. This acceptance has often been criticized by Christians as non-dynamic and static. The overcoming of desire leads to a simple non-demanding life style, a detachment from material things that bring only transient pleasures. Since modern Western economies are built on stimulating desires and acquiring material possessions as a way to happiness, they run completely counter to Buddhist teachings. In a way I understand the value of Western Capitalism because I fully realize that the wealth it has generated has been used in the medical sciences to relieve a great deal of physical suffering and pain. But keep in mind that despite the relief they provide, old age and death still have to be dealt with—either through acceptance or resistance to the end—when we will lose.

I recall a pathetic woman who was dying of cancer and she was almost skin and bones. She refused all mirrors in her room because she could not bear to see how she really looked. She was allowing all sorts of surgery to be performed in the hope of saving herself but which only debilitated her further while enriching the surgeons. Her existence was in the confines of a hospital room until she died. She could have accepted death and enjoyed her home with a staff to care for her and make her comfortable until the end. She only reinforced my beliefs.

Yet I would not like to live in a world as the one that existed at the time of the Buddha 2500 years ago. Modern technology and medicine have reinforced our blind hope in an eternal future. But even today, while we live freer of pain and suffering, the basic problems of life remain but are only delayed. While I enjoy the benefits of this century, I still adhere to the fundamentals of my religion and also deeply appreciate the medicines that permit me to survive in comfort.

BUDDHISM AND OTHER PHILOSOPHIES

About 100 year earlier than the Buddha, Lao Tsu of China expounded the philosophy of "The Way" (Taoism) which stated that it is not where we are going but the way in which we go that is important. "The Way is the End and the End is the Way." This introspective philosophy stimulated a quiet meditative life style. *How* you did something was more important that *what* you did. He was a teacher to Kung Fu Tsu (Confucius) who evolved the philosophy of harmony in all things that one does. Harmonious relationships in a family led to harmonious relationship with friends and strangers which led to harmonious relations with government which in turn led to a benevolent government made up of like-minded people. Wisdom and harmony went together as one had to learn and be wise to do what was right. The philosophies of Taoism and Confucism ruled China for centuries. They too taught the need for gracefully living and dying without struggling for survival in the face of hopeless odds.

Buddhism was introduced into China about the 2nd century of the present era. It blended perfectly with Taoism and Confucism. Around the 11th century, Japanese Buddhist missionaries went back to China to learn Buddhism from the masters ("ex cathedra"). It was during that period that the combined philosophies of Buddhism, Taoism and Confucism were pervading China as one religion which the Japanese missionaries brought back to Japan as Zen Buddhism. It still flowers today and has formed the art and life style of the Japanese people. It is practiced as an austere and peaceful way of life exemplified in the Tea Ceremony (the emphasis is on the way in which tea is served, not on what is being done). No one has expressed Zen philosophy and Zen way of life better that Kakuzo Okakura (Tensin) in his classic "The Book of Tea." In it, he describes the acceptance and gracefulness of living and dying. In particular he describes the great tea master, Rikyu, who was given the alternative to commit Hari Kari or be beheaded because the emperor Hideoshi believed court tumors that Rikyu intended to poison his cup of tea. Suspicion was enough to condemn someone to death. He accepted his untimely death sentence gracefully, gathered a few friends in his favorite tea house, read a poem he had written for the occasion and, with quiet dignity, took his life.

While Japanese are Mahayana Buddhists, we sense no difference in our beliefs. Moreover, their practice of Buddhism as it pervades their life is so profound that those who have encountered it have been deeply influenced ever after. When I think of death and dying, my thoughts go to their beliefs and traditions: Acceptance of pain, suffering and death is so deeply ingrained in their character that one cannot help but appreciate how natural all aspects of life are. We learn from them that change is universal and we all flow with that change.

Whether or not one is a Buddhist one can practice a life style of serenity and simplicity which is based on the Buddhist principles of acceptance of the Four Noble Truths and the Eight Fold Path. Everyone can approach old age and death gracefully without the pain and suffering that desire adds to these changes.

CONCLUSION

Like many people, I realize that at my age I too am old and facing death. But long ago, I leaned to deal with old age and death so that they are not strangers to be fought but friends to be accepted. I face my impermanence with the same feeling I face any new phase of my life and hope that you can do the same.

—Josef Kolenski

NEUROSCIENCE AND AGEING

Marcus Tullius Cicero (106-43BC) was one of the greatest Romans of all time; he was a statesman, writer, orator, and skillful politician. This book is dedicated to him and his wonderful treatise, *De Senectute* (*On Old Age*), an essay that has had an impact throughout the western world for over twenty centuries. His thoughtful treatise deserves a special place in literature—for its wisdom and perspective are marvelous; many of his ideas are extraordinarily still pertinent. However, the art of ageing and ageing well is still uncertain, even centuries later. We will review some of Cicero's early observations and add some additional perspective from the twenty-first century. As a seasoned practitioner and student of psychiatry and neurology in the golden decade of neuroscience, I will offer some new recommendations for your consideration.

Many mysteries of mind and body and the mind's connection to body remain unknown. Each human individual has his/her own fingerprints, and genetic potential; life's experiences and/or accidents can unmask or generate an uniquely artful life history.

Cicero addressed his tract on age and the ageing process (which was coming on apace) to a childhood friend in an effort to lighten the common burden for both of them. In the process he wrote that the composition of the tract itself was so delightful that it wiped away the annoyance and even made ageing a happy time for him.

We all can still derive many positive benefits from his artful essay.

"Age...far from being feeble and inactive is even busy and is always doing and effecting something—something of the nature as were in pursuits of earlier years."

Cicero and other classical philosophers especially had a profound and early influence in their immediate community and then later in many church writings a thousand years afterwards, even though those writings were not monotheistic. All Cicero's speeches and essays contributed to his worldly reputation as a good and wise man. Subsequently writers and philosophers from Chaucer, Petrarch, Erasmus, Montaigne to John Lock, David Hume, Kant and Schiller owed some debt in style, form and substance to this extraordinary human being. His life was even imitated by Anthony Trollope. He was also well studied by John Adams and the entire Adams family. There is no question that Ciceronian ideals affected the writers of the American Constitution, which has certainly aged well, as did so many of its authors.

Cicero's advice might be synthesized in nine recommendations:

> *Learn to cope with loss*
> *Maintain optimism*

Exercise memory by learning something every day
Surround yourself with the enthusiasm of youth
Exercise moderately and enjoy an active leisure
Be sociable and maintain friendships
Learn agriculture
Be grateful for loss of sexual desire
Enjoy your role as a mentor of others
Like faithful sentries do not quit your post until God, our Captain, calls.

1. The Losses of Ageing:

Cicero started his writing on the particular topic of ageing in his sixties, just following the death of his beloved daughter Tullia and his loss of his Senatorial role. Cicero had been excluded from his activities in Rome by Caesar's dominance in the court and in the Senate. In the course of his exegesis, he comments on the strength of a parent who can accept the loss of a child. The loss or serious illness of a child is an unique stress, and can certainly accelerate ageing.

At the time of the loss of his daughter, Cicero retired to one of his several villas outside of Rome. There he had the luxury of time and place to think deeply about time—the time in his life, his family life and also particularly his time out of government. (He never did recover his government role and was later assassinated.) In his quiet country place he was able to write as a relief from his troubles—and in his struggle to deal with his double grief. At the time he left the question of immortality somewhat uncertain, but he did state clearly that he hoped to meet friends in the afterlife. Ultimately, he felt that his life was good and that he was not born in vain. Certainly he ended on a most optimistic note, a clear resolution of his sadness.

With the acquisition of the art of ageing akin to other arts, each life is idiosyncratic and unpredictable. Regardless of genes, environment, diet, belief systems, we must expect the unexpected as we age. I include a few unique vignettes from my psychiatric experience to illustrate that many individuals have lived "artfully" in Ciceronian terms.

I am distantly related to the M family where an artful matriarch ruled for decades. From the M-family recently, I received an invitation and attended an unusual wedding in Boston. The great grandmother (Super M) of the groom was aged 105 (one of the two last survivors of 5 children). Her mother had lived to 98 (born in Russia)—but lived and died in Pittsburgh.

The great grandmother's outlook was generally optimistic, spirituality generous, active socially and active physically, taking walks alone regularly—up to 2 miles a day. She had married, was widowed, passed through the phases of motherhood, and grand motherhood with equanimity. She was always gracefully attired, dressed well, impeccably groomed, and an attractive petite dark-haired woman.

Super M had always participated in exercise classes daily, played bridge daily; she was called "stubborn" or "tenacious" by the family and friends. One day in her late 70's, she broke her hip and refused treatment for 36 hours because she had to go to an important dinner where she was to receive a public award. She felt that her private pain could wait and public acclaim was the priority. Stoic and extremely bright, she was always interested in others.

At the wedding I attended, she remarkably marched down the aisle with aplomb at the age of 105 as if she were a West Point cadet. She had always had one martini before dinner and did so before the wedding. She also walked in a sprightly manner after the ceremony and easily engaged in conversation. Prior to this encounter I had never met a woman of 105 years of age.

After the ceremony, I sat down with her and proceeded with some tactful questions about her life experiences and her family. She did have a younger sister aged 99 who was well. Presuming that she mastered a number of stressful episodes in her life, I asked about the "single most difficult event" for her. Without a moment's hesitation, she told me about her daughter's illness. She remarked about her daughter's failing memory and lack of activity; the "child" had had a stroke at 75. Ultimately, she proceeded to tell me about her struggle to put her "demented" daughter in a nursing home where the "child" had died within six months. As with every other story, she was remarkably free of visible grief or remorse.

Super M herself ultimately died at the end of her 106th year. Her exercise and bridge remained daily activities until the last weeks of her last year of her life. When her physician had tried to make an appointment in her 106th year, she refused, citing her busy daily schedule. "No" she could not make an afternoon appointment—she had a bridge game; "no" she could not make a morning appointment, she had an exercise class and a swimming routine.

He finally got an appointment with her and encouraged her to have an operation for a newly detected stomach cancer; she refused. She had been in an assisted living home for approximately two years. She died there in a matter of weeks—refusing hospitalization to the end.

Her life long physical and mental activity is a requisite that Cicero would have applauded. Her courage in facing her daughter's illness and death was striking. To quote Cicero, "many are the remarkable things I have observed in a great man (a friend of his who had become a distinguished general), but nothing more than the manner in which he bore the death of his son...."

2. The Joys of Ageing:

Cicero emphasized his positivism in his joy of ageing—citing his genuine love of conversation. The E family presented an aspect of this art. "Nothing is more excellent than intellect"...

Early on in life, E was a prodigious reader, first in her class to learn, and she frequently read to her entire class. She was entrusted at age eight with taking care of a little girl (aged 3) in her father's tenement building. Later as a teenager, she was further entrusted with the responsibility as head of a whole playground for 200-300 children.

During her senior year in high school, she won a full scholarship to Radcliffe (now Harvard) College at a time when there were few such opportunities available. Close to her graduation, she married a successful builder-entrepreneur. Shortly after the birth of her first child (a boy), her husband died in a horrible, fateful construction site accident. His body was so mutilated she never viewed it after the fateful day. A few years later the young widow was on the Atlantic beach with her young son where she met a young physician. He was enamored of the child and smitten by the new widow. Her new husband's family unfortunately did not welcome her. Although there were many rebuffs by his family, she remained steadfast in the marriage. She learned to avoid the most troublesome members of the new family and only contacted those who offered her some affection.

Subsequently she had a second child, a girl, and thereafter developed her own career in music. Later in life her new husband developed a serious recurrent major depressive condition which again tested her mettle in another arena. The relationship between stepson and her husband became filled with much tension, bickering and ultimately rejection. The boy moved overseas to go to college, but the conflict with his stepfather continued—such that he did not attend the stepfather's funeral.

E was an intrepid traveler and she remained so, visiting Europe with regularity and alone, into her mid 90's. At her 100th birthday, she wrote a monograph with her family entitled, "Celebrating the First One Hundred Years". With her special whimsy, she states in the second sentence, "I was a bit of a rotten kid." Grandparents were available and loving while she was growing up—as was a musically talented Uncle.

Her initial family home was opposite a theater. Although she did not actually attend many performances she was frequently told stories about the performances. Another uncle was a great raconteur. Later on she did go to many shows at another ethnic Yiddish theater.

E has never had any major medical problems except for some mile high blood pressure late in life. Now 102, she continues to love children, even though she has no grandchildren nearby. Her reading habits persist with the help of special glasses and a nip of bourbon at bedtime. She has friends half her age with whom she converses; and with whom she exercises regularly. Until last year she attended dance classes three to four times a week. Last year she perambulated through Harvard Yard in the alumni procession as the oldest living alumna.

She currently lives alone on weekends in the same apartment where she has lived for over 35 years; she is of perpetual good nature and is always ready to talk; she also delights in holding and playing with the baby of one of her aide care-givers; and she watches the CNN news daily and hopes to make a trip to London this year. Her grace in adversity remains an inexplicable gift. Perhaps her early exposure to stories of comedy and tragedy in the theater helped her learn that there are good days and bad days and both are to be treated with equanimity.

Cicero encouraged activity especially as one ages. Active leisure was his recommendation and this next example would please Marcus Cicero. "A sedentary life is hazardous" and he never recommended retirement.

We know the risk for obesity, diabetes, hypertension, and vascular disease. Sometimes hyperactivity that is unfocused can be illness behavior. However, goal directed action that is intense and consistent can and often does lead to great success. Early on success with activity is applauded and all would agree that active leisure today is included in artful ageing.

3. The Discipline of Ageing:

Cicero advocated keeping the mind taught like a well-strung bow. "One should keep command of one's household....Like the pilot of the ship, a statesman's judgment is crucial and one can, on reflection, insist that the others climb the masts, run on the gangways, work the pumps while he sits quietly at the stern and simply holds the tiller."

HB is such a man who has been winning awards and accolades into his 90's. His imagination created and produced radio programs of all sorts; later he moved into television and CD production. He was the first-born of four children. He had the marvelous good fortune to have both parents healthy into their 90's. As a brilliant student he graduated college and got a law degree in five years. He was shrewd enough to have bought life insurance annuities that are still paying off and supporting him. A gregarious fellow he was interested early in radio, first as an announcer and then a writer.

Born in Brownsville, he remained in and around New York his entire life, and is still producing programs. Most recently, he presented his Law School with a DVD (of his making) of their illustrious alumnus in the Supreme Court, Louis Brandeis. He created a whole series of radio programs including *Inner Sanctum, Bulldog Drummond, Dick Tracy, the Thin Man,* etc. Currently HB has six grandchildren and four great grandchildren. Once divorced and once a widower, he has now comfortably lived in his solitude for seven years. He is hardly solitary, however, for he regales his friends with stories about himself and his triumphs and awards. He has built friendships and has learned to take care of others and his siblings as he cared for his aged parents for many years. Although he has a certain braggadocio, he understands the Ciceronian meaning of friendship. HB has clearly remained the pilot of his ship!

"Real friendship is even more important than kinship; for the latter may exist without good will, whereas friendship can do no such thing. Friendship is the greatest of all gifts the gods bestowed on mankind…. Some give preference to riches or good health or power or public honor…Many rank sensuous pleasures highest of all. But feelings of that kind which any animal can experience, and the other items are transient and uncertain." Savoring friendships is one of the greatest pleasures to enhance ageing.

HB has organized festivals and anniversary parties for other friends and organizations. At this time in his life, he has a fabulous collection of paintings and has many fabulous friends. His numerous affiliations provide more social engagements and lively conversations than he can handle. His only recent stress is the onset of some legal action about relatives quarreling over their financial share in his success.

4. Requirements for Ageing Well:

"Just as we need the prime necessities of life…fire and water…we need friendship. Take away the bond of friendly (kindly) feeling from the world and no house, no city can stand."

In a separate tract, Cicero wrote specifically about friendship, but he always included that friends were crucial in ageing well. There are precursors to the capacity for friendship which are basic trust, a sense of humor, and a capacity for joy. These qualities permit subjective life satisfaction and are the foundations for successful and graceful ageing.

A. Bonding:

The role of bonding in survival is a source of ongoing ageing researches. Solitary individuals tend to have significantly shorter lives that those who have companions. Marriage or living with partners in a cooperative setting unequivocally helps to prolong life and add to the quality of the life lived.

(1) The Bonds of Music:

During the fall of 2004, at a Reading University, England workshop on music, language and human evolution, a writer suggested that a way of getting "high" with one's peers was via music. He argued that music lubricates bonding and thus survival. Is music then an important element in long life?

The earliest musical instruments created and played by humans appeared 32,000 years ago. There were flutes made of bird bones, according to some archeologists. It is likely, say other scientists that there may be genes for musicality that evolved and may go back 150,000 years ago.

Other researchers suggest that music might have evolved as a way for parents to sooth babies while foraging for food. Regardless of the outcome of the current investigations, social cohesion certainly seems essential for survival and cooperation. Group singing and dancing helps bridge what Dunbar calls the "endorphin" gap. Listening to music can does trigger the production of those feel good proteins (endorphins).

Darwin proposed another view: that music evolved to facilitate and was the result of sexual selection. He was making observations about male bird songs used to attract a mate and ensure reproductive success. Perhaps humans evolved the ability to sing to each other to express love, friendship and camaraderie. There are well known senior musicians who play joyfully until late in life, and I personally and without hesitation believe that music prolongs life.

At a seminar a decade ago on the biology of music making at the University of Rochester and the Eastman School of Music, longevity was analyzed in solo music fans versus symphony members. The morbidity and mortality among union musician members who retired and stopped playing at a fixed age was far greater than those individuals who continued their joyful playing or teaching. Hence, there is preliminary evidence that music was a plus in their personal and social evolution and my have been a significant factor in their longevity. The bonds of music certainly enhance friendship, mentorship and camaraderie.

(2) The Patient-Doctor Bond:

Another important dimension of personality is the capacity to "learn" to become a good patient, the kind of patient that a doctor can care for. Medicine had dramatically increased life span. In the past century, three decades have been added to average life expectancy. The change in life expectancy is partly due to specific public health measures. Another tremendous change is the availability of spare parts—transplants of hearts and lungs, bone marrow, etc. Replacements of hips, knees, heart valves and dental implants affect quality of life as well. In addition, it is also valuable to learn from your doctor how to be a good doctor for yourself. Physical and mental health are best maintained with objective social supports in the health care province.

B. Openness to New Ideas and New Activities

A 78-year old retired Indian UN official was suffering from Parkinson's disease, a potentially debilitating neurological and mental disease. During the early state of his illness, he had become withdrawn following the start of his retirement. His illness limited his physical activity which in turn impaired any desire to participate socially. His voice also weakened somewhat—so it became difficult to speak on the phone for any sustained time. His youthful gregarious nature seemed to have withered away. With his doctor's suggestions and wife's encouragement, a new "window" opened when he began to learn how to use a computer. Now he could communicate around the globe with his family in India and many former colleagues. A dramatic reawakening occurred and has been sustained.

A talented woman artist, mother of three (close to 80 years old) with many gallery shows to her credit, decided to embark on a new direction with her work—developing a different series of perspectives and different paints to enhance her career evolution. She had suffered through her husband's long illness and death with remarkable resiliency. Despite a family history of suicide and depression, she soldiered onward in inventing her new artistic style. She had spent a summer in an artists' colony where she was encouraged to experiment. Her teacher-mentor provided the crucial encouragement to follow a new path.

A retired manufacturer in his 80's sold his shirt business just before the influx of foreign textiles. Although extraordinarily successful, he always felt he had to "feed his factories." The demands of his union workers and the demands of the large department stores drained him emotionally. He had always longed to do something other than "business".

Tragically, he had lost his only son to a drug overdose. He moved to Florida and started sculpture classes in a university setting with great zeal. He had always hoped to do something creative and artistic. He did achieve his goal and remained healthy for another decade.

A 75-year-old construction executive was fired peremptorily from a senior position, having worked extremely conscientiously for well over 35 years. He was especially distraught because he was dismissed after having just completed a major project under budget and on time. In this sudden and forced retirement, he converted his anger to "constructive" activity. He learned to play pool and joined a pool league team. He also learned to fly high-speed kites and joined a social discussion group for the first time in his life.

These individuals, late in life, had the capacity and courage to take on new ventures in their work and play. A famed advertising executive has been quoted as saying, "when you are through changing, you are through…with life".

5. Passion and Ageing:

'Age is devoid of sensual pleasure and be grateful for age taking it away, i.e., the desire for carnal pleasures hinders deliberation, is at war with reason, blindfolds the eyes, so to speak, and has no fellowship with virtue.'

Cicero's view of age is hardly consonant with the sensualist 21st century. Millions of men (150 million) through the world are buyers of *Viagra, Levitra,* and *Cialis* and are seeking erotic fulfillment.

WH is a 68-year-old professor of medicine who was denied emeritus status at his university. He noted flagging interest in his wife at this time. Consulting his internist, he found a mild increase in blood pressure. An antihypertensive drug was prescribed which further decreased libido. Historically, WH had a spell of homosexual concerns in adolescence when he was plagued with self-doubt. Brief psychoanalysis helped him with this crisis over a period of many months. With a reduction in blood pressure medicine, prescription of an antidepressant and a modest dose of *Viagra*, the situation improved dramatically. His sexual life was better than it had been in many years and his partner was pleased.

JH is a 55-year-old entrepreneur with a large family and a large family of businesses. He had some battles with his father earlier in life and controversy with his family at the time of his marriage. Obsession with his sexual performance dominated his thinking. He decided to try several medicines to enhance his libido. These concerns began to spread to fears about the medicines. His wife was angered by his use of the drugs; she felt her attractiveness and sexuality were in question.

Many men do not refill their prescriptions for the medicines fearing misinterpretation by a partner. Some only want the reassurance of the drugs without using them except for extramarital affairs. Also, some wives are "retired" from sexual activity and resent a partner's reawakened desires.

So although medical remedies are available for declining male capacity, libidinal desires vary in every partnership. Many couples enjoy continual desire; others find it as troublesome as Cicero. In a landmark case, the prestigious *New England Journal of Medicine* reported finding syphilis in a 90-year-old man. A report of this sort would have stunned Marcus Tullius Cicero.

6. The Fear of Death:

As an organizing force in all lives, early psychoanalysts, including Sigmund Freud, believed and many continue to believe that fear of death is the primary fear. Another critical belief involved a child's inability to grasp the meaning of death until early adolescence. Both of these theoretical constructs are patently not true if one takes into account clinical and personal experience. Certainly there are some children and adults who do have dominating psychical fears of death. Denial of death or actual fears of death have been presumed to be at the core of psychology and the basis of many treatises. However, most of these clichés and generalization are obviously false. Many individuals do approach death with equanimity.

The notion of "passing on" is a euphemism from early Christian Science belief according to some knowledgeable historians. Hence, in obituaries in Christian Science belief, one never dies, one merely passes on to another life. This belief is also true in other cultures and the notion of rebirth in a better or different life pleases many religionists.

There are those who advocate avoiding funerals or memorial services as substantial stressors as one ages and loses friends and family. However, there are joyous funerals and joyful memorial services.

So we might add to Cicero's recommendations:
Expect the unexpected
Build a large circle of young friends
Be open to new ideas and new activities
Use music and dance—perform and listen
Learn to be a good patient—and become your own doctor when possible
Eat your greens

And keep up to date with neuroscience.

—Ralph N. Wharton

AGEING
IN
CHINA

China is the most populous country in the world with a population of over 1.3 billion inhabitants. Since China began economic reform and adopted an open policy to the world in 1978, many major changes have taken place. China changed economic systems from a highly centralized economy to a market economy, resulting in major financial growth. In 2004, the GDP reached 13,651.5 billion RMB (US$1.645 billion), up by 9.5% over that of 2003. People's living standards have greatly improved. Life expectancy increased from 35 years old before the founding of the People's Republic in 1949 to the current level of 71.8 years. This essay will firstly describe the present situation of the ageing Chinese population; then discuss the status of Chinese elderly people, the impact of the ageing population on China, measures protecting senior citizens and, finally, offer some suggestions on how to promote the development of the elderly in China.

The Ageing Population of China

In 1992, recognition of the world's rapidly ageing population, the General Assembly of the United Nations designated the year 1999 as the International Year of Elderly People. At the end of 1999, China announced that it was becoming a society of ageing people. According to the standards of demography, the sign of an ageing society is when the elderly population (over 65 years old) reaches 7% and the median age is 30 years.

The index of the China population met this standard in the nationwide census in November of 2000. Thus China became an ageing society with a lower level of social and economic development.

Since the People's Republic of China came into existence in 1949, there have been five national censuses between 1953 and 2000. Table 1 shows the changes of Chinese population in age structure from those five censuses.

*

Table 1 Age Structure from the Five Census				
Census Year	Time	0-14 aged	Population (%) 15-64 aged	65 aged and over
1953	1	36.28	59.31	4.41
1964	2	40.69	55.75	3.56

(Continued)[*]

Table 1 Age Structure from the Five Census

1982	3	33.59	61.50	4.91
1990	4	27.69	66.74	5.57
2000	5	22.90	70.00	7.10

[*]   Source: Above information is from China's National Census Data in 1953, 1964,1982,1990,2000, National Census Office of the State Council, the People's Republic of China.

In the first Census in 1953, the age structure of the Chinese population was in a young-adult stage with 4.41% ageing population; but China had only 3.56% of an ageing population in the Second Census in 1964, indicating a young society. The Third Census data in 1982 showed an adult stage with an ageing population reaching 4.91%, and the Fourth Census data in 1990 indicated that China had grown into an adult-ageing population structure with the ageing population reaching 7.10%. So the speed of ageing in the Chinese population was accelerated, particularly in this decade. Table 2 shows the indexes of ageing in the recent three censuses. It shows that the ageing index and median age have been rising in recent decades and reached the standard of an ageing population in the Fifth Census in 2000. Moreover, recent statistical data from the National Statistic Office shows that in 2002 the population of the elderly amounted to 7.2% of the overall population in China and the median age climbed to 33.1 years. It seems that ageing people in China will be a constantly growing percentage in the future years. According to the prediction of some specialists, the Chinese elderly population will increase most rapidly between the years 2010 to 2035, and the number of senior citizens whose age is over 65 will rise by 0.6% per year. Forecasts by the United Nations show the Chinese ageing population peak will occur in the year 2040 reaching 18.3% and the median age would move up to 39.4 years.

*

Table 2 Indexes of Aging in Recent Three Times Censuses

Census Year	Time	Ageing Index	Median age (years old)
1982	3	39.92	22.65
1990	4	42.01	25.30
2000	5	45.51	30.85

[*]   Source: Chinese National Census Data in 1953, 1964, 1982, 1990, 2000, National Census Office of the State Council, the People's Republic of China.

Table 3 shows the distribution of Chinese elderly population in 2000. It indicates that the elderly over 65 years old exceeded 88 million. Among the ageing population, the rate of the female elderly was increasing from slightly over one half of the ageing population over 65 years old to two thirds of those over 85 years old. The population of the rural elderly was about as two times larger as that of the urban elderly, and also had a higher ageing level (average elderly population was 7.5% in rural areas while only 6.3% in urban areas.)

There are several reasons for the increase in the ageing population in China. One of the most important reasons is that the family planning program carried out in the 1970's resulted in a dramatically declining birth rate and accelerated the ageing population. Especially in 1979, the Chinese government made great efforts to advocate the fertility policy of "one couple, one child". Since then, the birth rate has declined greatly. In 1982, the birth rate was 22.28%, and it decreased to 13.38% in 2001. Another reason is the change of attitude in the Chinese people. For a long time in history, almost all the Chinese had a traditional notion that they would like to bear several children and expect to obtain support from their children when they are too old to take care of themselves.

*

Table 3 Distribution of Chinese Elderly Population in 2000

	Population (millions)		Female Rate (%)		Distribution (%)	
	65+	85+	65+	85+	65+	86+
	(years old)		(years old)		(years old)	
Urban	29.47	1.34	52.2	66.6	33.4	33.5
Rural	58.81	2.66	53.0	66.4	66.6	66.5
Total	88.28	4.00	52.8	66.4	100.0	100.0

*   Source: Chinese National Census Data in 1953, 1964, 1982, 1990, 2000, National Census Office of the State Council, the People's Republic of China.

But with the great progresses in social and economic development, the younger generations are different from their ancestors. Some even do not want to have children. The third reason is that the conditions of medical treatment have been greatly improved. Therefore, the death rate has declined and the average life expectancy has increased. As is shown in the statistic data, the death rate decreased from 20% in 1949 to 6.45% in 2000.

The speed of China's population ageing is extremely fast. In less than 40 years, the proportion of people aged 65 and over will increase from 7.1% in 2000 to 18.3% in 2040; it will take 80 years or more for such an increasing rate in developed countries. In addition, the distribution of the ageing population is imbalanced in China. It shows that the rural areas have a higher ageing growth than the urban. With younger laborers migrating to urban areas, the eastern region of China has a higher ageing population than the western region of China, consistent with the development level of the regions.

According to the 2000 census, 33.1% were still working but 67% had left the job market and stopped earning money. There was a significant difference in job rates between the rural and urban old people: 43% of the population over 60 years old in rural areas (male 54.9% and female 32.0%) were working to earn money and, on the contrary, only 13.4% of the population over 60 years old in urban areas (male 19.2% and female 8.0%) had jobs. With age rising, the laboring proportion of those over 65 declined, 32.9% in rural areas and only 9.4% in the urban areas. Differences in types of employment, the labor market, and the social security policy between rural and urban areas were the key reasons people left the job market (cf. Wang, W.G., Xu, Y., Li, Q.Y., 2004). Generally speaking, the retiring urban elderly have sounder social security programs and a better pension and have a relatively stable life level. But, without a social security system, most of the rural elderly have to labor even if their health is poor. Census data in 2000 showed that 60% of the urban elderly depended on a retirement pensions and basic living allowances to live on, and 40% depended on family support. However, only 10% rural elderly can get a retirement pension and basic living allowance, and more than 85% of the rural elderly rely on family sustenance. Compared with the male elderly, the proportion of female elderly who got retirement pensions and basic living allowances was only one-half of that of the males; the proportion of female elderly supported by their family members was two times high than the male elderly. As the census data indicates, the population in poverty accounted for 7.1% to 9.4% in the elderly in China with the poverty rate of the elderly in the countryside higher than that of the urban elderly (rural:8.6%~10.8%; urban: 4.2%~5.5%). In a self-assessment financial survey of the elderly, 4.5% of older people in urban and 8.2% older people in rural areas stated that they were in very poor economic situations. When asked about their level of contentment or happiness, 5.9% of older urban people and 10.2% of older rural people thought that they were comparatively unhappy in their old age (Wang, D.W., Zhang, K.T., 2005). It is clear that the poor elderly are mainly those who are sustained by their families, and so family poverty may be the main cause of such elder poverty. We can also conclude that poverty happening for rural older people is larger than that for the urban aged. The quality of life for the rural elderly is worse than for that of the urban. So only when the rural economy is developed and the economic burden of the rural families reduced will the quality of life improve for rural aged people.

Impact on China of an Ageing Population

China is a developing country that is growing into an ageing society before attaining first world status and having sufficient wealth. It is a nation "Getting Old before Being Rich". This special national situation brings challenges to the development of China and will result in some problems. As B. J. Xong showed in 2004, dependency ratio for the elderly was 15.4% in 2000, and will climb to 17.4% in 2010 and 24.7% in 2020; the dependency ratio will go up from 53.6% in 2010 to 55% in 2020. The Ministry of Labor and Social Security predicts a gap in the retirement pension payment program of about 100 billion RMB (c. US$12.5 billion) by the end of 2005; a nationwide research project indicates that the number of retirement pensions will be as 13 times larger in 2020 as in 2000. As Professor Huang has shown by the "growth factor" method, health expenditures increased 0.06 from 1990 to 2000 but will grow 1.96 from 2030 to 2040 before declining to a negative value of 0.08. His study indicates that the amount of population has little effect to the growth of health expenditure. However, during 2030 to 2040, the growth of health expenditure caused by an ageing population will reach the maximal value; from the year 2010, national health expenditure in China because of an ageing will grow more rapidly than the population and this trend will continue. Therefore the increase in health expenditures caused by an ageing population is estimated to be about 1% to 2% annually during 2010 to 2050.

Clearly the ageing population in China will increase some negative impact in social and economic development. However, as long as the Chinese face the challenge practically, and take countermeasures to deal with the problems caused by an ageing population, the negative impact could prove to be the opportunity to push China to enter a new course of development. Some options that could be adopted are as follows:

Some Remedies

1) Construct a National Social Security System. The existing social security system in China is "a combination of social pooling and individual accounts". But the social security system is now only for employees in urban areas and people in the countryside do not share in the program. However, even in cities the retirement pensions are significantly different due to the economic imbalances among various areas of China, (particularly between well-developed eastern China and undeveloped western China) and because of the different incomes determined by jobs and careers. In addition, people in state-owned organizations will be guaranteed a generous retirement pension offered by government. Despite government requirements, people in some private organizations might not get any retirement pension if their employers avoid payments. Facing an ageing population, China's social security system must be truly transformed and it has been suggested China organize a social security system which covers the whole country and allows the rural people to share in the benefits also. It should be a national priority to set up a rural social security system because the problem of poverty is mainly in rural areas. Professor Li showed that the one-child family policy in the 1970's decreased the labor force in rural areas greatly. Another reason that may cause the rural elderly losing family support is that many young people left home and migrated to the cities because of recent and rapid economic urban development. The migration of youth from rural areas has had some negative impact on the living arrangements of the elderly. It reduces the chances of the elderly living with and being supported by their sons according to the traditional Chinese view. Beginning a family aid program may prove to be a new way to solve some problems in the rural communities. A family aid program might provide cash or food to the family supporting the elderly; could reduce various taxes that the family must pay to the government if the elderly lives with and is cared for by the family; and could allocate land and residences to the elderly without family support which would revert to the government at the death of the tenant. Implementing it successfully needs legislation, which will guarantee the elderly actually getting economic benefits. However, the government's strong support and participation are important for the family aid program to proceed. The Chinese Central Government issued Document No. One at the beginning of 2005 spelling out further measures aimed at boosting rural income. It requires all provinces to eliminate the 8.4% farm tax; it mandates that at least 70% of any additional spending on health care and education be directed to rural areas; and it calls for an increase in subsidies and greater government investment in agriculture. If this new policy is implemented, the authors believe that elderly in the rural area will be getting better treatment. It is also urgent for the government to set up a national social security system in order to guarantee the rural elderly a sustainable life.

2) Develop New Support Systems. There ate two main support systems for the older persons in China: family support and community support. Family support is the traditional way and the most understood by the older people in China. Family support is confirmed by law and family members, especially sons and daughters, have the obligation to support their elderly by providing economic support, care and consolation. This traditional way is also accepted by the younger generation from the Chinese ethical view of respecting the elderly. Also community support has developed rapidly in the recent years. The once typical Chinese family of a younger couple together caring for their mutual parents and also their child is becoming a difficult role in the 21st century. In some communities today that have good housing and services, older persons now choose to remain at home or in a residence which reduces their children's burdens of caring for them. The older persons are familiar with the communities they live in and it is relatively convenient to remain in contact with their children. It is clear that this kind of social support will become a new and promising system as China enters into an ageing society. However, at present, family support is still the principal system in China, especially in rural areas where the other style has not been established. Perhaps combining the advantages of family care and community support will offer a better way to meet the emotional needs of the elderly and reduce the young couples' burdens. Developing and perfecting a viable community support system must be the future for China's ageing society.

3) Encourage Elder Consumerism. Currently the consumption share for the elderly is less than 0.5% of the whole n market. Obviously this proportion will change with the increasingly ageing population. Market investigation shows that 89% of the elderly are unsatisfied with the market. Researchers forecast that the elder market is potentially huge and will create a new leap in the Chinese economy. It is estimated that many of the elderly have significant purchasing power. So learning the various needs of the elderly and producing products to meet their tastes and needs will be a very effective way to promote the economic development of China. The keystones for an elder industry are health services and long-term care facilities (LTC). Recreation and physical equipment for the elderly are also needed to improve the quality of their life.

4) Increase Community Education. The chance of continuing education is a prior condition to becoming a mature society. Within Chinese traditional educational concepts, education in formal school or university has been regarded as the right of young people, not old persons. However, as we enter into a knowledge-based society, life-span access to education and training is very important for all individuals to learn new knowledge and skills, whether young or old. So the older persons need to accept continuous education and training if they want to participate in their societies. At present in China, there are about 17,000 senior citizen's universities or schools providing education for older persons. However, the number of the elderly in these kinds of schools only account for one to four percent of the ageing population in China. Over ninety percent of the elderly in China have not entered schools to enjoy this benefit. In some low economic areas as well as in the rural areas, the older person's right to such an education is often not available. Popularizing education for older persons and empowering them with equal educational opportunities regardless of their age, sex, region, or culture are the main and urgent issues to which the Chinese government gives priority. Many older people can acquire or enhance their abilities to develop themselves as their society develops and share in the benefits of social progress. However, considering that elderly will spend more time in their communities and are familiar with their environment, education should be offered in the older person's community.

Differences between the Urban and Rural Elderly

Although the government of China has made some countermeasures in dealing with the challenges of an ageing population, there have been great differences between the urban and the rural elderly in their chances of obtaining subsistence and development. Because of the major differences between their economic, social and cultural situations, the urban and rural persons go into their old age dissimilarly. The urban elderly usually can get a relatively better quality of life than the rural elderly in China. China can eliminate these differences between the urban and the rural elderly by:

1) Education. Most of the urban older persons have registered in elder schools or universities nearby their residences where curricula are available for the elderly, such as medical care, physical training, psychological health, nursing, painting and calligraphy, music, current affairs education and in computer training. Some are required courses and some are optional, and if the elderly finish the courses, they will get certificates when upon completion of the program. So the urban elderly have a continuing education after retirement. The older persons use the knowledge and skills learned from school to run a newspaper or magazine, hold exhibitions for their painting and calligraphy, set up internet elder schools, etc. which will serve society. Some Shanghai elderly even began to learn driving in school since the legal age of the driver is 70 years old in some local regulations. Obviously the educational content of the urban elderly should be arranged to be consistent with the needs of social development for the elderly. Furthermore, in some cities in China, distance education is offered to the elderly, so they can get instruction through TV at home. The rural elderly have not enough schools and there are not plenty of teaching tools (teachers, teaching materials and equipment such as computers) even if there is an elder school in their village. On the one hand, it is because of the poor local economy and, on the other hand, it is that the local governments have not realized the necessity and importance of elder education. Therefore many rural elder are neglected. However, in some rural areas with better local economic situations, elder education is beginning to be improved. Elder schools and training centers or classes for rural elderly in adult schools are gradually being built. For example, Haiyan, a county in Zhejiang Province, has established elder education programs focusing more on advanced agricultural technological knowledge and skills as well as usual courses. So it is believed that the future of rural elder education may be made in time comparable to urban.

2) Social Security Benefits. Social security is the most important guarantee for the older person's life. For the urban older persons, they share the retirement pension and can get steady economic income after they retire; whereas the rural elderly scarcely have a retirement pension because most of them have no jobs. So if they lose the ability to work, they have to be completely supported by their family members. The existing social security system has not covered peasants. Only 1.0% of peasants join Social Security, yet only 26.2% of rural elderly think they can support themselves (the proportion among the urban elderly is over 50%). To solve this problem for the rural elderly, some local governments take some measures to help the aged to broaden income sources when they come into old age. In Daxing district, a rural area near Beijing, a "general benefit system" has been created which adopts a fund-raising model with individual accounts and local government support for 246,000 farmers. Therefore the Daxing district peasants have got an endowed insurance income program for the first time. However, China still has a long way to make all the rural older persons obtain such an endowment insurance. As for service for the old, in urban places elder community services play an important role. For instance, the Zhabei district in Shanghai built three social networks for the elderly who live alone: The security net cares about and examines whether the elderly live in safe home environment with proper protection measures in hot and cold weather and whether the equipment the elderly used is in working order; assistance net serves the elderly who have difficulty in walking or going outside for shopping, cooking, bathing, etc.; the recreation net satisfies the needs of the elderly for seeing a film, participating in literary and physical activities, and sightseeing. With these three social networks running jointly, the elderly can obtain necessary help in time if a problem happens. So some sound social service systems for the elderly have begun in some urban areas. But in rural areas, though some rural community services have been set up, family members mainly offer health and social services to the elderly. Perhaps because of poverty or conflicts, elders may be abused by family members and may not get good care or treatment. Some rural elderly have died from neglect; some elders have chosen suicide because of depression.

3) **Leisure Opportunities.** The elderly should have a right to entertainment and recreational facilities. In urban areas, equipment is found in most communities. Playing chess, cards or mah-jong, reading newspapers and magazines and exercising are some of the recreational activities the elderly often do in the communities. Some elderly plant flowers, tend fish or raise birds at home; some elderly like to watch TV and listen to the radio; some like to visit their neighbors or friends; and some like to go sightseeing. In Guangzhou, a major city in south China, watching TV is the most popular entertainment for the elderly. Many urban older persons often take part in diversified activities organized by communities or folk organizations, such as in competition between communities in singing, dancing, or games to win honor for their communities; some 20% of elderly participate in some volunteer service to help needy people; and others prefer sightseeing around China to see the beautiful scenery. No doubt many urban elderly enjoy beneficial leisure time activities. On the contrary, older persons in rural areas lack such activities: They have fewer entertainment places and equipment (only 20% of rural communities have elder recreational rooms and only 14% have exercise areas for the elderly). Moreover, the rural elderly have not much time for any such recreation. Besides laboring in the field or at home, they often have to help to care for their grandchildren, especially when their parents immigrate to cities to work. Life tends to be difficult for the elderly, although it is always an important and happy benefit for them when grandchildren live with them and solidify family relationships. Generally speaking, some rural elderly are often supersti-

tious because of a poor education; some feel lonely; and some find life anxious due to conflicts with the younger generations and fear losing family support. So it is a great need to organize effective rural elder associations to help them and offer a place for them to socialize with each other, join in public activities and try to pursue a happy life.

4) **Re-employment.** After retirement re-employment is often found for the urban older persons who have professional knowledge and skills. Some of them are re-employed by their former companies or units; new units also employ some. These older persons generally have high academic degrees, advanced knowledge and skills in their field, such as professors and senior engineers in universities and research institutions. They may undertake research tasks for the society. Other older persons re-employed are advanced technological personnel who are greatly needed in the labor market today. Re-employment increases income for the elderly and improves the quality of their life. Besides, re-employment raises the enthusiasm of the elderly to participate in society and realize their social value which will enhance their feelings of happiness. In rural areas, if physical conditions permit, most of the elder persons still labor even if very old. On one side, the rural elderly can increase income; on the other side, it is an emotional factor since they love the land that is their life. Therefore they will work the property as long as they can.

In October 1996, China government enacted "The Assurance Law of Older Persons' Rights and Interests" to protect the older person's rights and interests. While the Chinese government passes such protective legislation, it is more important for the younger generations, particularly in the rural areas, to care and support their old people.

The Elderly as Human Resources

In the Second World Assembly on Ageing in 2002, five important principals for older persons were put forward by The United Nations. The assembly emphasized that it was an available and unique way to solve ageing issues by defining ageing as a major social development policy and promoting full integration and participation of older persons in society. The five principles are Independence, Participation, Care, Self-fulfillment and Dignity. The Independence Principle states that older persons should have access to basic services ability and care, opportunities to work or earn income, to choose retirement from the labor force, to have access to education and training opportunities, to have safe living environments and the support to reside at home as long as possible. The Participation Principle addresses decision making, dissemination of knowledge, community service and encourages associations of older person. The Care Principle discusses issues of family and community care, access to health, social and legal services, and matters pertaining to institutional care. The Self-fulfillment Principle calls for older persons to have opportunities for full development and access to educational, cultural, spiritual and recreational resources. The Dignity Principle talks about issues relating to exploitation, physical or mental abuse and fair treatment.

However, taking these principles into reality will require initiative from the older persons and the establishment of an enabling environment by the rest of society. Common myths about ageing marginalize older people and portray them as burdens to society. Contrary to this popular belief, older people contribute a lot to society, working in paid and unpaid jobs, providing shelter, food and education to children, caring for grandchildren, ailing spouses or other relatives and playing an active part in community life.

Older people have experience and wisdom. Older people are the precious treasure and resource of a society; they have made contributions to the development of the society in their younger age, and can also continue to offer their devotion to the progress of the society. As Cicero said older people leave their work when they lose the physical energy they used to possess when young. However, they could still do some work efficiently for the society. He further explained that it may not depend on physical strength and quickness if one seeks achievement, but on intelligence, prestige and affirmation. The older persons do not lack the latter traits. On the contrary, they can become more pre-eminent as their age increasing. So how to properly utilize the elderly as a particular human resource is a key and imminent problem that all nations with ageing populations must face and answer.

Older persons should be regarded as an important human resource for social development, not a burden on society. In the course of positively participating in social construction, the elderly experience a reaffirmation of self-value, confidence, and happiness and can create another splendid stage of life. Active participation in developing societies means older people continue to participate in the affairs of their nations and communities and contribute to their nations and societies.

On December 4, 2002, Shanghai won the bid to host of the 2010 World Expo. The news inspired all Chinese, especially those in Shanghai. The slogan "Better City, Better Life" was popularized by Shanghai citizens. Shanghai's development embodies China's desire to integrate into the international community with a robust economy, sound infrastructure, clean environment and social stability. Shanghai citizens like their city and wish to make it better by providing a better life for them. Shanghai had an elder population of 11.5% in the year 2000; over 97% of older people in Shanghai enroll in various kinds of senior citizen's schools or universities. In responding to Shanghai government's call for preparing for the Expo, lots of ordinary older people participated in campaigns to support Expo. Many older persons begin to learn English. They said: "Even if we just learn one word or one sentence in English every day, we can master thousands of words and sentences in English when the World Expo is held in the year 2010. Thus we can speak a little English and certainly can offer help to the foreigners coming to Shanghai if they are in need of aid." In China, more older persons actively take part in the construction and development of China and contribute their abilities and wisdom to their society. At the same time, they create a colorful, rich and meaningful old age life for themselves.

Eric Erikson, an American psychologist, described a life-span development in his psychosocial development stage theory. In his theory, he proposed eight stages in the human lifespan: Basic trust versus basic mistrust; autonomy versus shame and doubt; initiative versus guilt; industry versus inferiority; identity versus role confusion; intimacy versus isolation; generactivity versus stagnation; and ego integrity versus despair.

Each life stage has a twin conflict and then a core developmental task to complete. If an individual completes the core developmental task in an earlier life stage, he will experience positive emotions and enter into the subsequent life stage prepared to complete another developmental task. Older people enter into the eight-life stage, the last stage of human life. The conflict of this stage is called ego integrity versus despair, and the individual's task is to overcome the conflict and discover a perspective for his lifespan. If the older individual integrates himself well, he will actively participate in his final life station. If the old individual considers that his whole life was useless, he will feel desperate and angry. However, Erikson also stated that even if an individual did not do well in his earlier life stage, he would still have a chance to do well in the next life stage. He can begin a new life as long as he participates in society.

Now that China has turned into an ageing society, it is very urgent to find ways to make older people healthy and active. While society may improve the older person's life quality and encourage a meaningful and artistic old age, positive ageing must be carried out by the elderly themselves.

Some Ways Chinese People Can Enjoy an Active and Healthy Old Age

1) **Daily Exercise.** Having a healthy body is a basic condition. Older persons go through a heavy decline both in physical and mental level. Sometime older people feel that they become another person. To change this situation, they should exercise moderately every day. Exercise can produce a healthy body and a good mood. In China, many communities provide various equipment for exercises, and moreover, increasingly Chinese elderly begin to recognize the importance of exercise to their health and well being in old age. So it is very common to see in the early morning in every city of China, lots of older people doing all kinds of exercises in the park.

2) **Form a Senior Personality.** It is quite useful for older person to have a sound, healthy personality in old age. In the beginning years of the retirement, many old people seem to lose direction in their life. They do not know anything else in life except their previous work. In addition, the decline in physical and mental levels begins to happen. All these changes make it difficult for many old persons. Even some people who have good characters before they became elderly become unbelieving, obstinate and angry. They begin to lack confidence and are afraid to be looked down upon by family members. So shaping a sound elder character is a benefit for most old people. The first step is to help them recognize changes as quickly as possible and let them accept the changes as calmly as they can; and then instruct them to build a new life character in old-age. Having a direction of a new life, old people soon can develop positive attitudes to a new role in life and shape a good personality. In the senior citizens' schools and communities in China, many curricula and activities are arranged for the older persons to help them get rid of the negative feelings of old-age and build a new elder character.

3) **Foster Inter-Generational Relationships.** The theme of the International Day 2004 was "Older Persons in an Intergenerational Society". This theme recognized the important role that older people play in their families, communities and societies. Establishing an intimate relationship with the younger generation is not just good for older people, but also benefits the younger generation. For the

younger generation, a relationship with the elderly offers them knowledge and skills in life and in the workplace. As Cicero described: The younger generation love to mix in with wise older persons, and that the older persons, who are loved and esteemed by the younger generation, will become calm and easy; the younger generation then relies on the elderly much more because they can get instruction. Both generations obtain enjoyment in mixing with each other.

In China, one of our traditions is to esteem the elderly. This national traditional character is deeply planted in the heart of every Chinese. Thus it is easy to understand why family support is still accepted by both the elderly and the younger generations in modern times in China. In 1989, the Chinese Central Government designated the day of September 9 annually (according to Chinese lunar calendar) as "Senior Citizen's Day". Every year around that day, the local government officials, who are the representatives of the Central Government, will visit the elderly in their community and review their situation and living allowance. Moreover, every district has also designated a "Day of Helping Older Persons" which reminds the younger generation about the traditional commitment to the elderly. Most places have established volunteer service teams to help older persons with questions about the relevant laws, health programs, retirement benefits and home care. In the course of dealing with older persons, younger generations establish an intimate relationship with the elderly and vice versa which will be continued in Chinese society.

4) Participate in Social Affairs. Participating in society can reduce the loneliness of the elderly. By communicating with others in society, the elderly are easy to empathize with other people and build close relations with them. This feeling is important for them at this age and they will think that they are still useful to society though they are old. So it is usually found in China that the elderly have high spirits and more actively participate in social activities than any other social group. The 10th National Games of China were held in Nanjing in October of 2005. More than ten thousand older people in Nanjing performed Taiji (a kind of Chinese marital art) together during the opening. The older performers regard themselves as the representatives of all the older people in China and certainly should do their best for the National Games. So many Chinese elderly gain a meaningful and happy old life by participating positively in social activities.

5) Learn New Things. To learn new things is not only the needs of an individual, but also the need of a developing society. Today society in China is becoming a knowledge-based one. If one does not learn new knowledge, he or she will soon be abandoned by his society. Therefore, one of older people's important tasks is learning new things constantly. Maybe the elderly need more time than the younger generations in learning things, but as long as they have a desire to learn, older persons can master the new knowledge or new skills. It is definitely true that the older persons who like to learn new things and accept new things quickly are always wiser persons. Through learning constantly, older persons can grow with their society and they can utilize and share in the progress of their society. In China, teaching older persons new technological is just beginning. However, it is our belief that with the increase of elder schools, more and more Chinese older persons will acquire more new knowledge and new skills and elevate their life quality.

6) Offer Support Systems. In today's China community support has not developed well; many services for the older persons have not been started yet in communities. So mutual support highlights the inadequacy of community support. In Shanghai, Beijing and other big cities in China, some communities have established a mutual support system encouraging healthy elderly to help the oldest-old in their communities. The older people generally offer free caring and emotional consolation to the oldest-old. Because they consider that helping the oldest-old is a social obligation if their physical condition permits.

7) Accept Death. Cicero had said that the most natural and ordinary thing in the world is human death. Nature ends all life as a normal event. So the elderly need not worry about and be afraid of death. A wise older person scorns death and treats the coming of death with calmness. Active ageing in China includes making older persons accept the correct attitude toward death. Recognizing that death is inevitable, older persons will effectively arrange their life and social activities; they will especially cherish the days staying with their younger generation and trying to remember and share every piece of happiness with the families. At the same time, most of them will take part in social affairs. They hope they can contribute to their society. So everywhere in China, it is very easy to find lots of older persons join various activities held by their communities, local governments, and folk organizations. Most Chinese older persons have a positive attitude towards death. Some even ask their families to donate their bodies to the hospital for medical use after they die. They think that their bodies may be the last useful things that they could contribute to their society.

However, it is equally important to realize that Chinese society should play a key role in using the elderly as a special human resource. When we encourage older persons to achieve ageing positively, then they will realize their self-value and social value. China is just a beginning to carry out this project though we have gained some initial success. In the future China should take measures to advance the steps of developing the elderly as a human resource to promote positive age-ing.

Suggestions for Further Government Action

1) Mainstream the Elderly as a National Resource. The old, traditional world-wide view is that older persons are simply regarded as social burdens. But this conception is wrong and should be changed quickly because more and more countries are becoming ageing societies. Older persons are important and they are a part of the human resources of a society. They are full of experiences, virtue, knowledge and skills. The urgent thing now is to let every person, including the elderly themselves, realize the social and individual importance of the elderly and then the government should declare the elderly a national resource and part of its national development plans. Through this resource integration, all social factors will benefit. In China, the central government and local governments have begun to pay attention to developing senior citizens as a national resource, but much is yet to be done.

2) Adjust the Retirement Age. In China, the present retirement age is 60 years old for males and 55 years old for females. Some industries have an even earlier retirement. With China's economic growth and the development in medical care, most of the Chinese people at this retirement age are in good health and they are able to do their jobs competently. So moderately adjusting the national retire-ment age will benefit both individuals and society. Changing the retirement age by several years, perhaps 5 to 10 years, has great social and economic values as well as individual value. It will be necessary to consider this suggestion as popula-tion ageing in China becomes more serious in the near future.

3) Organize an Elder Human Resource Database. In order to effectively make use of the elderly as resources, the Department of Personnel in each organization or the Department of the Elderly should build up a database for the elderly and establish an information network so that society can better utilize their abilities and assist them in finding proper positions where they are needed. In addition to this, the government ought to set up personnel markets for the elderly. It is also important for the Department of Elderly Issues to set up a committee that con-sists of experts from different vocations to advise the government on its elder pol-icies. Therefore, human resource management of the elderly will prove to be a new field in China.

4) Offer Retraining Programs. The greatest social advantage of the elderly is their rich work experiences. However, if the elderly are re-employed, they certainly need to accept retraining for their new positions because of the rapid change of society. So establishing training programs would be a great help. In China, the importance of the utilization of the elderly has not been recognized. Some re-employed elderly assume consulting roles to teach young employees, but most of their experiences may be based on old situations which are different from the situations of today. So lack of advanced knowledge is always a disadvantage. Generally speaking, schools for the elderly in China teach more knowledge on health care than that of modern technical knowledge. it is urgent for the senior citizen's schools to add curricula of advanced knowledge and skills for those who want to be properly re-employed in the workplace.

5) Meet the Needs of the Elderly. Whenever working with older persons, it is vital for an organizer to realize the situations and needs of the elderly. All activities for older persons should embody the principle of being "Older People Centered". That is to say that the workload for the elderly should not be very heavy, otherwise it may affect their health. China plans to use the elderly as a resource in an effective long-term manner and many Chinese elderly want to be employed again if only for one-third of their previous compensation.

6) Recognize Problems of the Female Elderly. The female elderly in China have a longer life expectancy than the male elderly. The average life expectancy of the male rose from age 68.06 in 1995 to age 68.81 in 2000, whereas the female increased from 71.82 in 1995 to 73.06 in 2000. The life expectancy of the female is higher for about 4-6 years than that of the male in the corresponding period after the year 2000. Therefore, in the future, China must manage and utilize the female elderly well in the development of society. Because of the traditional sex role of the female in China, the rate of illiteracy is higher than that of the male elderly and they have lower or no retirement pension. Thus a number of female elderly in China, especially those in rural areas, are living in poverty or and most of them are supported by their families. Therefore, Chinese society must find effective ways to help the female elderly to achieve good living conditions and enjoy a happy and active life

The Time of Beautiful Flowers

The proper development and integration of older persons into Chinese society will be a great challenge to the central Government of China. China is a developing country and is an ageing society at the same time. This special national situation needs all of the Chinese to work with their government to make great efforts to complete the giant task of such integration in this new century. To put the eld-

erly into a social development plan to achieve positive ageing is very urgent matter for the Chinese government—and all Chinese including the elderly
themselves. From the view of individual development, it is demanded that the
Chinese elderly should participate in their society actively and create a happy,
healthy, and meaningful life; from the view of social development, it is required
that a careful social plan for the elderly should be mapped out in order to manage
and utilize them better as an important national resource. Such a program will
also give the **elderly a better and more meaningful life by encouraging them
to make a contribution to society.**

Old age is a season of harvest, wisdom, wealth and maturity. The Chinese like to
compare the elderly to the setting sun which while going down still has beautiful
rays of light. Therefore, a song sung for lauding the elderly: "Nothing is more
beautiful than the setting sun. It is warm and quiet. It is just like beautiful flowers
opening late, and it is also like pure wine intoxicating people". Cicero said that a
person should acquire the habit of being kind and honest, especially when elderly. So building a meaningful life is actually an art not just for the elderly but
also for people of all ages. Maintaining good health, being happy and construct-
ing an active social life are the artful elements required to acquire a contented old
age.

—Shuming Zhao and Huifang Yang

References:

>Cicero (Marcus Tullius Cicero, 106-43 BC), *Old Age, Friendships and Duties,*
    from *Cicero: Selected Works*, London,: Penquin Books, 1984. The Chinese
    version was translated by D. Gao & F. Zhang and published by Shanghai
    Sanlian Bookstore, 1989.

>Huang, C.L. (2004), "The effect of ageing population on the growth of health
    expenditure." *Chinese Journal of Population Science, No. 4, 36-43*

>Lai, D.S., Tian, Y.P. (2004), "Social Security and human capital investment",
    Chinese Journal of Population Science, No.2, 13-21

>Li, J.M.(2004)." Study on social security for the once family planned elderly
    couples in rural China.," *Chinese Journal of Population Science, No. 3, 40-
    48.*

>Lugo, J. (1990). *Lifespan Development.* Translated by Chen, D.M., Xuelin Press, 1997.

>Mu, G.Z. (2002). "On old-age development," *Population Research, 26(6 29-37.*

>Poston, D.L. & Gu, B.Ch.(2005), "The effects of the fertility and mortality transitions on the elderly and elder care in China," *Chinese Journal of Population Science, No.1,* 42-49.

>Shang, Y.& Yu, W.H.(2004), "Research on mobile phone market and product for the adult and the old," http://www.dolcn.com/data/cns 1/article 31/paper 311/pind 3111/2004-11/1100606617.html, 2004.11.16

>Song, J.G.Song, W.J. (2002). "Focusing of the older population and building healthy ageing in China," *Medicine and Society, Vol. 15(6),*35-36.

>Tai, E.P., *etal.*(2002). "Life quality of the elderly in China in investigation in the urban and rural areas," http://www.cnca.org. en?include/content.asp?thing id=10506

>Wang, D.W., Zhang, K.T. (2005), "The Chinese elderly: how they live and how many of them are in poverty," *Chinese Journal of Population Science, No.1,*59-66.

>Wang, S.J. (2002). "How about the life of the elderly?" http://www.snweb.com/gb/people daily/2002/12/13k1231001.htm

>Wang, W.G., Xu, Y., Li, Q.Y. (2004), "Quantitative analysis on change of age structure to development of economy," *Market & Demographic Analysis, 10(6),*1-8.

>Venne, R. (2002)," Mainstreaming the concerns of older persons into the social development agenda," http://www.un.org/esa/socdev/ageing/documents/positionpaper.pdf

> Xong, B., Yang, J.R. (2002)," Population ageing and human resource exploiting of older persons in China," *Journal of Chongqing Institute of Technology, 16(3),*7-9.

>Xong, B.J.(2004), "How to face the challenge of population ageing in the course of building the well-to do society," *Journal of Pinguan University, 21(2),*4-6.

>Yang, Y.N.(2005), "The family-aid program: A study on the tactics of improving the rural families' function of old-security," *Population & Economics, 148(1),*44-47.

>Yuan, Y.L.(2003). "China population ageing and analysis on elderly market," *Business Economy, No.10,* 13-15.

>Zeng, Y., & Wang, Z.L.(2004), "Family and changes of living arrangement of the elderly in China," *Chinese Journal of Population Science, No.5,*2-8.

>Zhang, B.B.(2002), "Analysis on social and economic aftereffect and policy selection under China population ageing," *Macro-economy Review, 40(3),* 27-33.

>Zhang, W..J., & Li, S.Z.(2004), "Determinants of rural elderly living arrangement under the context of labor migration," *Chinese Journal of Population Science, No. 1,*42-49.

> Zhang, Z.B. (2005), "Research on health situation of rural elderly in west China," http://www.cpirc.org.cn/yjwx detail.asp?id=2445

>Zhao, S.M. *Human Resource management in China,* Nanjing University Press, 1995.

>Zhong, Y.L.; Yan, Z.Q. (2000),"The leisure life style of senior citizens among big cities—features and suggestions.," *Market and Demographic Analysis, Vol.6(4), 69-71.*

>Zhou, S., Zhang, L.H. (1998), "A comparative study on physical and psychological health of 201 aged students before and after entering the university for the old," *Medicine and Society, Vo., 11(5)*35-36.

CHAPTER TWO

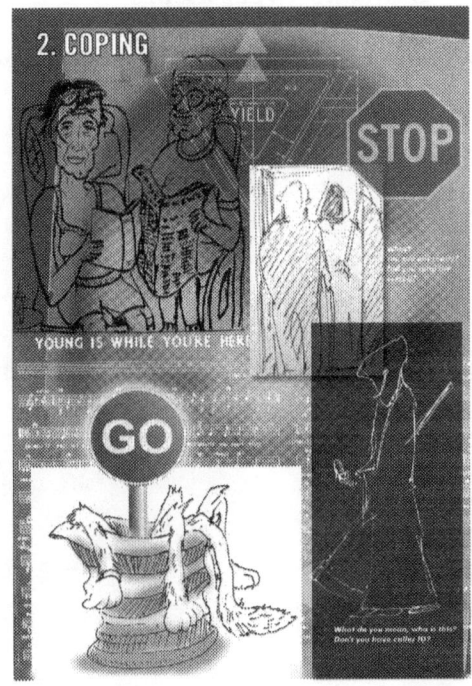

COPING

Senescence begins
And middle age ends,
The day your descendants
Outnumber your friends.

I Wouldn't Have Missed It: Selected Poems
By
Ogden Nash
(1975)

Young is While You're Here;
Old is When You're Gone.

"If you compliment me on being wise…it is because I regard nature as the best guide."

—Cicero, *On Old Age* (Bk. I).

At the age of 85, I have reached many conclusions about things that mystified me 50 years ago. No two people age at exactly the same pace nor is it all due to genetics. My wife, at 82, is still more beautiful than most women of forty. I am more youthful than most men of 70. An accident? Hardly.

For almost 23 years we have been adherents to the regimen worked out by a genius name Nathan Pritikin. He was an inventor, credited with having been the leading force in the creation of the Norden bombsight. This clever instrument made overland bombing "smart" many years before the invention of the "smart bomb" of today. Mr. P suffered a massive heart attack when he was about 40 years old. Doctors told him he would be chair-and-bed bound for the rest of his life; Nathan would not accept that.

Because of his success with the bombsight, he was given access to files he wished to examine—not only in this country but, more pertinent to his theories, to that of the U.K. Over there, he looked for the increase of heart attack during WWII since the medical profession places so much emphasis on stress as a key factor in the development of cardiac breakdown. He discovered that the rate of heart attack plummeted during the war. He wondered, beyond the stress theory, what effect deprivation of the "wholesome foods" such as milk, eggs, butter and red meats had on the population only to find that it had little harmful effect.

Thereupon he gained access to cadavers of people who died of heart attack since the war and discovered that there was plaque in their coronary arteries. An analysis of the consistency of that plaque revealed fat and something new to him: *cholesterol*. Then he pursued the presence of this new finding in red meats, eggs and milk products and found both cholesterol and fat in differing amounts.

Using himself as a guinea pig, he eliminated red meats, eggs and milk fats from his diet. At the same time, he began walking every day—starting with two blocks and increasing it every day. The doctors warned him that he would kill himself with this new program but he disagreed and soon began jogging! After a few weeks he was running a few miles every day—and no heart attack. But, in the scientific experimentation, he decided that this program of diet and exercise had to be tried with others. But where to find the candidates? Nathan found the answer in the lost souls of California, wine-guzzling alcoholics.

He billeted these men in a rude house he bought for the purpose and saw to it that they ate only the foods he provided. In addition he started them on an exercise program of walking and, later, running. The neighbors, who had objected strenuously to the introduction of what they termed riffraff into their community, observed a marked change within a month and no longer raised any objections. The former winos were no longer pale, filthy and listless, but ruddy, active and clean looking.

Pritikin also reasoned that, since the human mouth has more molars for grinding than simple tearing teeth, they must have been destined for chewing grains and vegetables.

From these foods the body would thrive and not make cholesterol and fat deposits in the arterial system.

As a result of this success and validation of his new program, he started the first simple Pritikin Longevity Center. For the first time, this genius offered a new concept of a meatless, dairy-fatless, but plentiful grain and green vegetables to the world. In addition he urged that drinking fruit juices be replaced by eating the whole fruit. In that way we ingest the fruit fiber, which, in addition to proper diet, is another way of clearing the arteries and veins that the fiber passed through. He began with only a few paying customers. But the news of Type Two diabetics being cured at his institute and of people who entered on canes, crutches and wheelchairs getting rid of them within a week or two at the most (like Lourdes) spread quickly. It was not hearsay—we were there and we saw these modern miracles. In spite of doctors, to whom illness is good business, *warning patients against entering this new institute*, its fame persuaded many to begin the pilgrimage to Santa Monica to see for themselves.

That's why Edith and I also persuaded ourselves that this was the new way to go. And our health today speaks volumes for the Pritikin regimen. We eat his way and exercise his way. In spite of the fact that, in 1940 when I was called up by the Army draft, I was rejected as unfit to serve because of what they called a bad heart (the effects of scarlet fever, a once vicious disease, when I was a child), here I am at 85. No accident. Pritikin!

Besides that, Edith has a phrase that encompasses the attitude of many who survive 'til the later years but do not care for themselves as they did forty years earlier and look like crones—she says: "They *embrace* old age." I believe she's absolutely right. Here's our further advice to them: *"Don't embrace old age!"* Inside, most of us feel much as we did in our youth; then display that feeling *outside*! Don't put a number on when you're supposed to suddenly age.

I have spent my life (and still do) writing songs. Some became worldwide hits, like *"IT WAS A VERY GOOD YEAR."* Another was *"I BELIEVE."* Each had its own philosophy. In a like way, in a Broadway musical that I wrote, I created a number that ended the First Act. The title was *"The Things We Are Begin With What We Think We Are."* In another musical that I wrote which never reached Broadway, there was a song called *"Young Is While You're Here—Old Is When You're Gone!"* That's a healthy way to approach life. Edith and I would urge that, in your later years, you embrace youth. It's more fun, and you and everyone you know will feel better about you if you do. Grow older without growing old. Have fun!

—Ervin Drake

"YOUNG IS WHILE YOU'RE HERE"

If your body gives respectable heat,
If your heart still makes detectable beat,
Conclusion is that you're not getting on.
Young is while you're here. Old is when you're gone!

If you still have eyes for something in silk,
Pinch the nurse who brings you crackers and milk,
If in your legs there's one more Marathon,
Young is while you're here. Old is when you're gone!

While your position is perpendicular to ground,
While your condition is not particular unsound,
Say! It's nice to be around.
When the young men fly their rockets in space,
Lots of old men soon take over their place
And all the sweet young girls will write "Dear John:
Young is while you're here. Old is when you're gone."

Young is while you're here, Old is when you're gone.

—Ervin Drake

YOUNG IS WHILE YOU'RE HERE

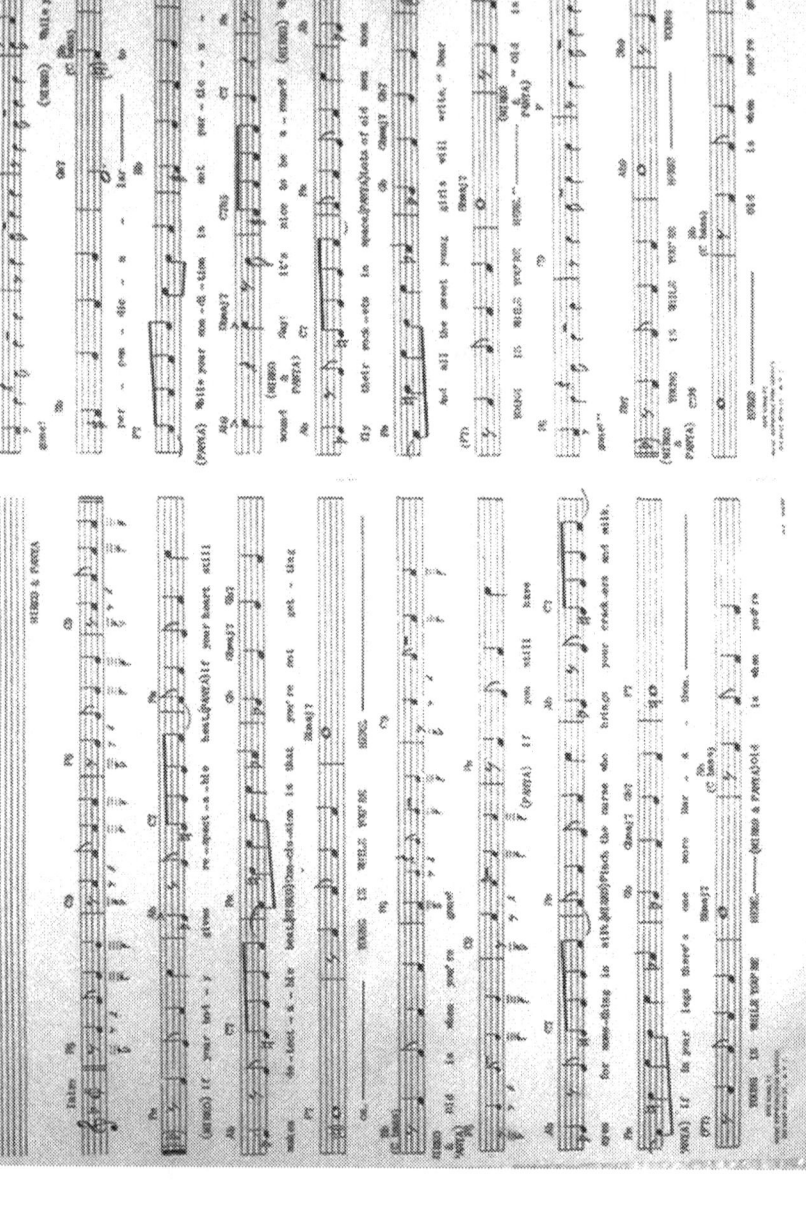

The Old Man and his Grandson

There was once a very old man, whose eyes had become dim, his ears dull of hearing, his knees trembled, and when he sat at table he could hardly hold his spoon, and spilt the broth upon the tablecloth or let it run out of his mouth. His son and his son's wife were disgusted at this, so the old grandfather at last had to sit in the corner behind the stove, and they gave him his food in an earthenware bowl, and not even enough of it. And he used to look toward the table with his eyes full of tears.

Once, too, his trembling hands could not hold the bowl, and it fell to the ground and broke. The young wife scolded him, but he said nothing and only sighed. Then they bought him a wooden bowl for a few halfpence, out of which he had to eat.

They were once sitting thus when the little grandson of four years old began to gather together some bits of wood upon the ground. "What are you doing there?" asked the father. "I am making a little trough," answered the child, "for father and mother to eat out of when I am big."

The man and his wife looked at each other for a while, and presently began to cry. Then they took the old grandfather to the table, and henceforth always let him eat with them, and likewise said nothing if he did spill a little of anything.

—Jacob and Wilhelm Grimm

"GRANDAD"

I've been sitting here all day thinking
Same old thing ten years away thinking
Now my days are gone, memories linger on
Thoughts of when I was a boy

Pennyfarthings on the street riding
Motorcars were funny things, frightening
Bow and hoops and spinning tops
Annie Gretzel's lollipops
Comic cuts, all different things

Grandad, granddad you're lovely
That's what we all think of you
Grandad granddad you're lovely
That's what we all think of you
Grandad grandad

Areoplanes tied up with string flying
Telephones and talking things sighing
A radio and phonograph, Charlie Chaplin made us laugh
Silently falling about
Familiar things I keep around, near me
Memories of my younger days, clearly
Now it's in my mind?
Everyday I find, thoughts of when I was boy

Grandad, granddad you're lovely
That's what we all think of you
Grandad, granddad you're lovely
That's what we all think of you
Grandad, granddad

Grandad, granddad

Grandad, granddad

—Clive Dunn
United Kingdom, 1971

(Internet Available)

THE CAT IN THE HAT

ON AGING

I cannot see
I cannot pee
I cannot chew
I cannot screw
Oh my god, what can I do?
My memory shrinks
My hearing stinks
No sense of smell
I look like hell
My mood is bad - can you tell?
My body's drooping
Have trouble pooping
The Golden Years
hace come at last
The Golden Years
can kiss my ass.

The Goldens' Age

"Some people never stop learning, however old they are…the aged (Athenian statesman) Solon wrote poetry…(the philosopher) Socrates in old age learnt to play the lyre…and, now 84, I have learnt to read Greek."

—Cicero, *On Old Age* (Bk. II)

CHAPTER THREE

TESTIMONIALS

"With all due deference to Mr. Cicero, old age is a vile thing."

Ivan Turgenev to Gustave Flaubert, 18 July 1872, *Turgenev Letters* (1983), when 54 years old.

A LETTER TO THE ELDERLY

To My Elderly Brothers and Sisters:

Seventy is the sum of our years,
or eighty if we are strong,
and most of them are fruitless toil,
for they pass quickly and we drift away. (Ps. 90:10)

1.Seventy years was an advanced age when the Psalmist wrote these words, and few people lived beyond it. Nowadays, thanks to medical progress and improved social and economic conditions, life expectancy has increased significantly in many parts of the world. Still, it remains true that the years pass quickly, and the gift of life, for all the effort and pain it involves, is too beautiful and precious for us ever to grow tired of it.

As an older person myself, I have felt the desire to engage in a conversation with you. I do so first of all by thanking God for the gifts and the opportunities which he has abundantly bestowed upon me up to now. In my memory I recall the stages of my life, which is bound up with the history of much of this century, and I see before me the faces of countless people, some particularly dear to me: They remind me of ordinary and extraordinary events, of happy times and of situations touched by suffering. Above all else, though, I see outstretched the provident and merciful hand of God the Father, who "cares in the best way possible for all that exists"[1] and who "hears us whenever we ask for anything according to his will" (1 *Jn* 5:14). With the Psalmist, I say to him: "You have taught me, O God, from my youth and till the present I proclaim your wondrous deeds. And now that I am old and grey, O God, forsake me not, till I proclaim your strength to every generation that is to come" (*Ps.* 71:17-18).

My thoughts turn with affection to all of you, dear elderly people of all languages and cultures. I am writing this letter to you in the year which the United Nations Organization has appropriately wished to dedicate to the elderly, in order to direct the attention of society as a whole to the situation of all those who, because of the burden of their years, often have to face a variety of difficult problems.

In this regard the Pontifical Council for the Laity has offered some helpful points for reflection.[2] In this Letter I wish simply to express my spiritual closeness to you as someone who, with the passing of the years, has come to a deeper personal understanding of this phase of life and consequently feels a need for closer contact with other people of his own age, so that we can reflect together on the things we have in common. I place all this before the eyes of God who embraces us with his love and who sustains us and guides us by his providence.

2. Dear brothers and sisters, at our age it is natural to revisit the past in order to attempt a sort of assessment. This retrospective gaze makes possible a more serene and objective evaluation of persons and situations we have met along the way. The passage of time helps us to see our experiences in a clearer light and softens their painful side. Sadly, struggles and tribulations are very much a part of everyone's life. Sometimes it is a matter of problems and sufferings which can sorely test our mental and physical resistance, and perhaps even shake our faith. But experience teaches that daily difficulties, by God's grace, often contribute to people's growth and to the forging of their character.

Beyond single events, the reflection which first comes to mind has to do with the inexorable passage of time. "Time flies irretrievably", as the ancient Latin poet put it.[3] Man is immersed in time; he is born, lives and dies within time. Birth establishes one date, the first of his life, and death another, the last: The "alpha" and the "omega", the beginning and end of his history on earth. The Christian tradition has emphasized this by inscribing these two letters of the Greek alphabet on tombstones.

But if the life of each of us is limited and fragile, we are consoled by the thought that, by virtue of our spiritual souls, we will survive beyond death itself. Moreover, faith opens us to a "hope that does not disappoint" (cf. *Rom.* 5:5), placing us before the perspective of the final resurrection. It is not coincidence that the Church, at the solemn Easter Vigil, uses the same two Greek letters in reference to Christ who lives yesterday, today and forever: He is "the beginning and the end, Alpha and Omega. All time belongs to him and all the ages.[4] Human experience, although subject to time, is set by Christ against the horizon of immortality. He "became a man among men, in order to join the beginning to the end, man to God".[5]

A Complex Century Towards a Future of Hope

3. In speaking to the elderly, I know I am speaking to and about people who have made a long journey (cf. *Wis.* 4:13). I am speaking to my contemporaries, and so I can readily draw an analogy from my own personal experience. Our life, dear

brothers and sisters, has been situated by Providence in this twentieth century, which arrived with a complex inheritance from the past and has witnessed many extraordinary events.

Like so many other times in history, our own has registered lights and shadows. Not all has been bleak. Many positive aspects have counterbalanced the negative, or have emerged from the negative as a beneficial reaction on the part of the collective consciousness. Yet it is true too—and it would be both unjust and dangerous to forget it!—that unprecedented sufferings have affected the lives of millions and millions of people. We need but think of the conflicts which erupted on different continents as a result of territorial disputes between States or inter-ethnic hatred. Nor should we consider any less serious the conditions of extreme poverty afflicting broad segments of society in the Southern Hemisphere, or the shameful phenomenon of racial discrimination and the systematic violation of human rights found in many nations. And what are we to say of the great global conflicts?

In the first part of the century there were two of them, with casualties and destruction never previously known. The First World War killed millions of soldiers and civilians, cutting off so many human lives in adolescence or even childhood. And what of the Second World War? Breaking out after a few decades of relative peace in the world, especially in Europe, it was even more tragic than the first, with enormous consequences for the lives of nations and continents. It was all-out war, an unheard-of-mobilization of hatred, which struck brutal blows even against defenseless civil populations and which destroyed entire generations. The toll paid on various fronts to the madness of war was incalculable; equally terrifying was the slaughter which took place in the death camps, which truly remain the Golgothas of our time. The second half of the century was burdened for long years by the nightmare of the cold war, the conflict between two great opposing ideological blocs, East and West. This was accompanied by an insane arms race and the constant threat of an atomic war capable of bringing humanity to extinction.[6] Thank God, that dark page of history was closed with the fall in Europe of oppressive totalitarian regimes as the result of a peaceful struggle, which relied on the weapons of truth and justice.[7] This in turn initiated a difficult but fruitful process of dialogue and reconciliation aimed at establishing a serene and fraternal coexistence between peoples.

But all too many nations are still very far from enjoying the benefits of peace and freedom. In recent months great concern has been caused by the outbreak of violent conflict in the Balkans, which had earlier been the theatre of a terrible war with ethnic undertones. Further blood was shed, further destruction took place, further hatred was nourished. Now that the clash of arms has at last ceased, thought is being given to reconstruction as the new millennium approaches. But meanwhile, on other continents too, numerous hotbeds of war continue to erupt, at times with massacres and acts of violence which are all too soon forgotten by the world press.

4. While these memories and these painful happenings sadden us, we cannot forget that our century has also seen the appearance of many positive signs which represent so many sources of hope for the Third Millennium. There has been a growing consciousness—albeit amid numerous inconsistencies, especially where respect for the life of each human being is concerned—of universal human rights, proclaimed in solemn and binding international declarations.

Moreover, there has been a continuing development of a sense of the right of peoples to self-government in the context of national and international relations, inspired by an appreciation of cultural identity together with respect of minorities. The fall of totalitarian systems, like those of Eastern Europe, has led to growth in the universal perception of the value of democracy and of the free market, although the great challenge of uniting freedom and social justice still remains.

We must also consider it a great gift of God that the world's religions are striving with ever greater determination to carry on a dialogue which would make them a fundamental factor of peace and unity in the world.

Then too, there has been an increasing recognition of the dignity of women. Undeniably there is still far to go, but the trail has been blazed. A further reason for hope is the rapid expansion of communications which, thanks to present-day technology, have made it possible to reach beyond established borders, making us feel that we are citizens of the world.

Another important area of growth is the new ecological awareness which deserves encouragement. Another source of hope is the great progress made in medicine and contribution of science to human well-being.

There are many reasons, then, for giving thanks to God. All things considered, these final years of our century present immense potential for peace and progress. From the very adversities which our generation has experienced, there comes a light which can brighten the years of our old age. Here we see the confirmation of a principle central to the Christian faith: "Tribulations not only do not destroy hope; they are its foundation".[8]

It is appealing, then, that, as this century and this millennium approach their twilight and the dawn of a new season for humanity can already be seen on the horizon, we should stop to meditate on how quickly time flies, not in order to resign ourselves to an inexorable fate, but rather to make full use of the years we still have before us.

The Autumn of Life

5. What is old age? At times it has been referred to the autumn of life—so Cicero calls it[9]—following the analogy suggested by the seasons and the successive phases of nature. We need but look at the changes taking place in the landscape over the course of the year, on the mountains and in the plains, in the meadows, valleys and forests, in the trees and plants. There is a close resemblance between our human bio-rhythms and the natural cycles of which we are a part.

At the same time however man is set apart from all other realities around him, precisely because he is a person. Made in the image and likeness of God, he is conscious and responsible. Even in his spiritual dimension, though, he experiences the succession of different phases, all equally fleeting. Saint Ephrem the Syrian liked to compare our life to the fingers of a hand, both to emphasize that its length is no more than a span, and to indicate that each phase of life, like the different fingers, has its particular character, and "the fingers represent the five steps by which man advances."[10]

Consequently, whereas childhood and youth are the times when the human person is being formed and is completely directed towards the future, and—in coming to appreciate his own abilities—makes plans for adulthood, old age is not without its own benefits. As Saint Jerome observes, with the quieting of the passions, it "increases wisdom, and brings more mature counsels".[11] In a certain sense, it is the season for that wisdom which generally comes from experience, since "time is a great teacher".[12] The prayer of the Psalmist is well known: "Teach us to number our days aright, that we may gain wisdom of heart" (*Ps.* 90:12).

The Elderly in Sacred Scripture

6. "Youth and the dawn of life are vanity", observes the Preacher (*Ec.* 11:10). The Bible does not hesitate to point out, at times with blunt realism, the fleeting nature of life and the inexorable passage of time: "Vanity of vanities...vanity of vanities, all is vanity" (*Ec.* 1:2). Who is not familiar with this stern warning of the ancient Sage? Those of us who are older, schooled as we are by experience, understand it in a special way.

Despite such wry realism, Scripture maintains a very positive vision of the value of life. Man remains forever made "in the image of God" (cf. *Gen.* 1: 26), and each stage of life has its own beauty and its own tasks. Indeed, in the word of God, old age is so highly esteemed that long life is seen as a sign of divine favour (cf. *Gen.* 11:10-32). In the case of Abraham, in whom the privilege of old age is stressed, this favour takes the form of a promise. "I will make of you a great nation, and I will bless you and make your name great. I will bless those who bless you and him who curses you I will curse, in you all the families of the earth will be blessed" (*Gen.* 12:2-3). At Abraham's side is Sarah, a woman who sees her body growing old, yet experiences within the limitations of her ageing flesh the power of God who makes good every human shortcoming.

Moses too was an old man when God entrusted him with the mission of leading the Chosen People out of Egypt. It was not in his youth but in his old age that, at the Lord's command, he did mighty deeds on behalf of Israel. Among other examples of elderly people in the Bible, I would mention Tobit, who humbly and courageously resolved to keep God's Law, to help the needy and to endure blindness patiently, until the angel of God intervened to set his situation aright (cf. *Tob.* 3:16-17). There is also Eleazar, whose martyrdom bore witness to an exceptional generosity and strength (cf 2 *Macc.* 6:18-31).

7. The New Testament, filled with the light of Christ, also contains eloquent examples of elderly people. The Gospel of Luke begins by introducing a married couple "advanced in years" (1:7): Elizabeth and Zechariah, the parents of John the Baptist. The Lord's mercy reaches out to them (cg. *Lk.*1:5-25, 39-79). Zechariah, already an old man, is told that a son will be born to him. He himself makes the point: "I am an old man and my wife is well on in years" (*Lk.* 1:18). During

Mary's visitation, her elderly kinswoman Elizabeth, filled with the Holy Spirit, exclaims: "Blessed are you among women and blessed is the fruit of your womb!" (*Lk.* 1:42), and when John the Baptist is born, Zechariah gives voice to the Benedictus. Here we see a remarkable older couple, filled with a deep spirit of prayer.

In the Temple at Jerusalem, Mary and Joseph bring Jesus to offer him to the Lord, or rather, in accordance with the Law, to redeem him as their first-born son. There they meet the aged Simeon, who had long awaited the Messiah. Taking the child in his arms, Simeon blesses God and proclaims the Nunc Dimittis: "Lord, now let your servant depart in peace" (*Lk.* 2:29).

At Simeon's side we find Anna, a widow of eighty-four, a frequent visitor to the Temple, who now has the joy of seeing Jesus. The Evangelist tells us that "she began to praise God and spoke of the child to all who were looking for the redemption of Jerusalem"
(*Lk.* 2:38).

Nicodemus too, a highly regarded member of the Sanhedrin, was an elderly man. He visited Jesus by night in order not to be seen. To him the Divine Teacher reveals that he is the Son of God who has come to save the world (cf. *Jn.* 3:21). Nicodemus appears again at the burial of Jesus, when, bringing a mixture of myrrh and aloes, he overcomes his fear and shows himself a disciple of the Crucified Lord (cf. *Jn.* 19:38-40). How reassuring are all these examples! They remind us that at every stage of life the Lord can ask each of us to contribute what talents we have. The service of the Gospel has nothing to do with age!

And what shall we say of Peter in his old age, called to bear witness to his faith by martyrdom? Jesus had once said to him: "When you were young you girded yourself and walked where you would; but when you are old, you will stretch out your hands, and another will gird you and carry you where you do not wish to go" (*Jn.* 21:18). These are words which, as the Successor of Peter, touch me personally; they make me feel strongly the need to reach out and grasp the hands of Christ, in obedience to his command: "Follow me!" (*Jn.* 21:19).

8. As if to recapitulate the splendid images of elderly people found throughout the Bible, Psalm 92 proclaims: "The just will flourish like the palm-tree, and grow like a Lebanon cedar..., still bearing fruit when they are old, still full of sap, still green, to proclaim that the Lord is just" (vv. 13, 15-16). Echoing the Psalm-

ist, the Apostle Paul writes in his Letter to Titus: "Bid the older men be temperate, serious, sensible, sound in faith, in love, and in patience. Bid the older women likewise to live in a way appropriate to believers...; they are to teach what is good, and so train the young women to love their husbands and children" (2:2-5).

Thus the teaching and language of the Bible present old age as a "favourable time" for bringing life to its fulfillment and, in God's plan for each person, as a time when everything comes together and enables us better to grasp life's meaning and to attain "wisdom of heart". "An honourable old age comes not with the passing of time", observes the Book of Wisdom, "nor can it be measured in terms of years; rather, understanding is the hoary crown for men, and an unsullied life, the attainment of old age" (4:8-9). Old age is the final stage of human maturity and a sign of God's blessing.

Guardians of Shared Memory

9. In the past, great respect was shown to the elderly. "Great was once the reverence given to a hoary head", says Ovid, the Latin poet.[13] Centuries earlier, the Greek poet Phocylides had admonished: "Respect grey hair: give to the elderly sage the same signs of respect that you give your own father".[14]

And what of today? If we stop to consider the current situation, we see that among some peoples old age is esteemed and valued, while among others this is much less the case, due to a mentality which gives priority to immediate human usefulness and productivity. Such an attitude frequently leads to contempt for the later years of life, while older people themselves are led to wonder whether their lives are still worthwhile.

It has come to the point where euthanasia is increasingly put forward as a solution for difficult situations. Unfortunately, in recent years the idea of euthanasia has lost for many people the sense of horror which it naturally awakens in those who have a sense of respect for life. Certainly it can happen that, when grave illness involves unbearable suffering, the sick are tempted to despair and their loved ones or those responsible for their care feel compelled by a misguided compassion to consider the solution of "an easy death" as something reasonable. Here it should be kept in mind that the moral law allows the rejection of "aggressive medical treatment"[15] and makes obligatory only those forms of treatment which fall within the normal requirements of medical care, which in the case of terminal illness seeks primarily to alleviate pain. But euthanasia, understood as directly causing death, is another thing entirely. Regardless of intentions and circumstances, euthanasia is always an intrinsically evil act, a violation of God's law and an offence against the dignity of the human person.[16]

10. There is an urgent need to recover a correct perspective on life as a whole. The correct perspective is that of eternity, for which life at every phase is a meaningful preparation. Old age too has a proper role to play in this process of gradual maturing along the path to eternity. And this process of maturing cannot but benefit the larger society of which the elderly person is a part.

Elderly people help us to see human affairs with greater wisdom, because life's vicissitudes have brought them knowledge and maturity. They are the guardians of our collective memory, and thus the privileged interpreters of that body of ideals and common values which support and guide life in society. To exclude the elderly is in a sense to deny the past, in which the present is firmly rooted, in the name of a modernity without memory. Precisely because of their mature experience, the elderly are able to offer young people precious advice and guidance.

In view of all this, the signs of human frailty which are clearly connected with advanced age become a summons to the mutual dependence and indispensable solidarity which link the different generations, inasmuch as every person needs others and draws enrichment from the gifts and charisms of all.

Here the reflections of a poet dear to me are pertinent: "It is not the future alone which is eternal, not the future alone!...Indeed the past too is the age of eternity: Nothing which has already happened will come back today as it was...It will return, but as Idea; it will not return as itself".[17]

Honour Your Father and Mother

11. Why then should we not continue to give the elderly the respect which the sound traditions of many cultures on every continent have prized so highly? For peoples influenced by the Bible, the point of reference through the centuries has been the commandment of the Decalogue: "Honour your father and mother", a duty which for that matter is universally recognized. The full and consistent application of this commandment has not only been a source of the love of children for their parents, but it has also forged the strong link which exists between the generations. Where this commandment is accepted and faithfully observed,

there is little danger that older people will be regarded as a useless and trouble-some burden.

The same commandment also teaches respect for those who have gone before us and for all the good which they have done: the words "father and mother" point to the past, to the bond between generations which makes possible the very exist-ence of a people. In the two versions found in the Bible (cf. *Ex.* 20:2-17; *Dt.*5:6-21), this divine commandment is the first of those inscribed on the second Tablet of the Law, which deals with the duties of human beings towards one another and towards society. Furthermore, it is the only commandment to which a prom-ise is attached: "Honour your father and mother, so that your days in the land which the Lord your God gives you may be long" (*Ex.* 20:12, cf *Dt.* 5:16).

12. "Rise in the presence of one with grey hair; honour the person of the older man" (*Lev.* 19:32). Honouring older people involves a threefold duty: Welcom-ing them, helping them and making good use of their qualities. In many places this happens almost spontaneously, as the result of long-standing custom. Else-where, and especially in the more economically advanced nations, there needs to be a reversal of the current trend, to ensure that elderly people can grow old with dignity, without having to fear that they will end up no longer counting for any-thing. There must be a growing conviction that a fully human civilization shows respect and love for the elderly, so that despite their diminishing strength they feel a vital part of society. Cicero himself noted that "the burden of age is lighter for those who feel respected and loved by the young".[18]

Furthermore, while the human spirit has some part in the process of bodily age-ing, in some way it remains ever young if it is constantly turned towards eternity. This experience of enduring youthfulness becomes all the more powerful when to the inner witness of a good conscience is joined the sympathetic concern and grateful affection of loved ones. Then, as Saint Gregory of Nazianzus writes, a man "will not grow old in spirit, but will accept dissolution as the moment fixed for the freedom which must come. Gently he will cross into the beyond, where there is neither youth nor old age, but where all are perfect in spiritual matu-rity".[19]

We are all familiar with examples of elderly people who remain amazingly youth-ful and vigorous in spirit. Those coming into contact with them find their words an inspiration and their example a source of comfort. May society use to their full potential those elderly people who in some parts of the world—I think especially of Africa—are rightly esteemed as "living encyclopaedias" of wisdom, guardians of an inestimable treasure of human and spiritual experiences. While they tend to need physical assistance, it is equally true that in their old age the elderly are able to offer guidance and support to the young people as they face the future and prepare to set out along life's paths.

While speaking of older people, I would also say a word to the young, to invite them to remain close to the elderly. Dear young people, I urge you to do this with great love and generosity. Older people can give you much more than you can imagine. The Book of Sirach offers this advice: "Do not disregard what older people say, because they too have learnt from their parents" (8:9); "Attend the meetings with older people. Is there one who is wise? Spend time with him (6:34); for "wisdom is becoming to the elderly" (25:5).

13. The Christian community can receive much from the serene presence of older people. I think first of all in terms of evangelization: Its effectiveness does not depend principally on technical expertise. In how many families are grandchildren taught the rudiments of the faith by their grandparents! There are many other areas where the elderly can make a beneficial contribution. The Spirit acts as and where he wills, and quite frequently he employs human means which seem of little account in the eyes of the world. How many people find understanding and comfort from elderly people who may be lonely or ill and yet are able to instill courage by their loving advice, their silent prayers, or their witness of suffering borne with patient acceptance! At the very time when their physical energies and their level of activity are decreasing, these brothers and sisters of ours become all the more precious in the mysterious plan of Providence.

In addition to the obvious psychological need of the elderly themselves, the most natural place to spend one's old age continues to be the environment in which one feels most "at home", among family members, acquaintances and friends, where one can still make oneself useful. As the number of older people increases, keeping pace with the rise in average life expectancy, it will become more and more important to promote a widespread attitude of acceptance and appreciation of the elderly, and not relegate them to the fringes. The ideal is still for the elderly to remain within the family, with the guarantee of effective social assistance for the greater needs which age or illness entail.

On the other hand, there are situations where circumstances suggest or demand that they be admitted to "homes for the elderly" where they can enjoy the company of others and receive specialized care. Such institutions are indeed praiseworthy, and experience shows that they provide a valuable service when they are inspired not only by organizational efficiency but also by loving concern. Everything becomes easier when each elderly resident is helped by family, friends and parish communities to feel loved and still useful to society. How can we fail to mention here, with admiration and gratitude, the Religious Congregations and volunteer groups specifically devoted to the care of the aged, especially the poor, the abandoned and those in difficulty?

Dear elderly friends who feel insecure because of ill health or other circumstances, I assure you of my closeness and affection. When God permits us to suffer because of illness, loneliness or other reasons associated with old age, he always gives us the grace and strength to unite ourselves with greater love to the sacrifice of his Son and to share ever more fully in his plan of salvation. Let us be convinced of this: He is our Father, a Father rich in love and mercy!

My thoughts turn in a special way to you, widows and widowers, who find yourselves alone in the final part of your lives; to you, elderly men and women Religious, who for long years have faithfully served the cause of the Kingdom of Heaven, and to you, dear brother Priests and Bishops, who, for reasons of age, no longer have direct responsibility for pastoral ministry. The Church still needs you. She appreciates the services which you may wish to provide in many areas of the apostolate; she counts on the support of your longer periods of prayer, she counts on your advice born of experience; and she is enriched by your daily witness to the Gospel.

You Show Me the Path of Life, in Your Presence There is Fullness of Life. (Ps. 16:11)

14. It is natural that, as the years pass, we should increasingly consider our "twilight". If nothing else, we are reminded of it by the very fact that the ranks of our family members, friends and acquaintances grow ever thinner; we become aware of this in a number of ways, when for example we attend family reunions, gatherings of our childhood friends, classmates from school and university, or former colleagues from the military or the seminary. The line separating life and death runs through our communities and moves inexorably nearer to each of us. If life

is a pilgrimage towards our heavenly home, then old age is the most natural time to look towards the threshold of eternity.

And yet, even we elderly people find it hard to resign ourselves to the prospect of making this passage. In our human condition touched by sin, death presents a certain dark side which cannot but bring sadness and fear. How could it be otherwise? Man has been made for life, whereas death—as Scripture tells us from its very pages (cg. *Gen.* 2-3)—was not part of God's original plan but came about as a consequence of sin, as a result of "the devil's envy" (*Wis.* 2:24). It is understandable why, when faced with this dark reality, man instinctively rebels. In this regard it is significant that Jesus, "who in every respect has been tempted as we are, yet without sin" (*Heb.* 4;15), also experienced fear in the face of death: "Father, if it be possible, let this cup pass from me" (*Mt.* 26:39). How can we forget his tears at the tomb of his friend Lazarus, despite the fact that he was about to raise him from the dead (cf. *Jn.* 11:35)? However rationally comprehensible death may be from a biological standpoint, it is not possible to experience it as something "natural". This would contradict man's deepest instincts. As the Council observed: "It is in the face of death that the riddle of human existence becomes most acute. Not only is man tormented by pain and by the advancing deterioration of his body, but even more so by a dread of perpetual extinction".[20] This anguish would indeed be inconsolable were death complete destruction, the end of everything. Death thus forces men and women to ask themselves fundamental questions about the meaning of life itself. What is on the other side of the shadowy wall of death? Does death represent the definitive end of life or does something lie beyond it?

15. Human history, from the most ancient times down to our own day, has provided a number of simplistic answers which limit life to what we experience on earth. In the Old Testament itself, certain passages in the Book of Ecclesiastes seem to present old age as a building in ruins and death as its final and utter destruction (cf. 12:1-7). But precisely against the backdrop of these pessimistic attitudes there shines forth the hope-filled outlook present in revelation as a whole and particularly in the Gospel: "God is not God of the dead, but of the living" (cf. *Lk.* 20:38). The Apostle Paul affirms that God, who gives life to the dead (cf. *Rom.* 4:17), will also give life to our mortal bodies (cf. ibid., 8:11). And Jesus says of himself: "I am the resurrection and the life; he who believes in me, though he die, yet shall he live, and whoever lives and believes in me shall never die (*Jn.* 11:26-26).

Christ, having crossed the threshold of death, has revealed the life which lies beyond this frontier, in that uncharted "territory" which is eternity. He is the first witness of eternal life; in him human hope is shown to be filled with immortality. "The sadness of death gives way to the bright promise of immortality".[21] These words, which the Church's Liturgy offers as a consolation to believers as they bid farewell to their loved ones, are followed by a proclamation of hope: "Lord, for your faithful people life is changed, not ended. When the body of our earthly dwelling lies in death we gain an everlasting dwelling place in heaven".[22] In Christ, death—tragic and disconcerting as it is—is redeemed and transformed; it is even revealed as a "sister" who leads us to the arms of our Father.[23]

16. Faith thus illuminates the mystery of death and brings serenity to old age, now no longer considered and lived passively as the expectation of a calamity but rather as a promise-filled approach to the goal of full maturity. These are years to be lived with a sense of trusting abandonment into the hands of God, our provident and merciful Father. It is a time to be used creatively for deepening our spiritual life through more fervent prayer and commitment to the service of our brothers and sisters in charity.

Most commendable then are all those social programs enabling the elderly to continue to attend to their physical well-being, their intellectual development and their personal relationships, as well as those enabling them to make themselves useful and to put their time, talents and experience at the service of others. In this way the capacity to enjoy life as God's primordial gift is preserved and increases. Such a capacity to enjoy life in no way conflicts with that desire for eternity which grows within people of deep spiritual experience, as the lives of the saints bear witness.

Here the Gospel reminds us of the words of the aged Simeon, who says he is ready to die now that he has held in his arms the long-awaited Messiah: "Lord, now you let your servant depart in peace, according to your word; for my eyes have seen your salvation" (*Lk.* 2:29-30). The Apostle Paul felt torn between the desire to continue living in order to preach the Gospel, and the desire "to depart and be with Christ" (*Phil.* 1:23). Saint Ignatius of Antioch, joyfully going to his martyrdom, said that he could hear within him the voice of the Spirit, like living "water" welling up inside of him and whispering the invitation: "Come to the Father".[24] These examples could be multiplied. They cast no doubt whatsoever on the value of earthly life, which is beautiful despite its limitations and sufferings, and which ought to be lived to its very end. At the same time they remind us that earthly life is not the ultimate value, in such a way that the twilight of life can be seen—from a Christian perspective—as a "passage", a bridge between one life and another, between the fragile and uncertain joy of this earth to that fullness of joy which the Lord holds in store for his faithful servants: "Enter into the joy of your master" (*Mt.* 25:21).

An Encouragement to Live Life to the Full

17. In this spirit, dear elderly brothers and sisters, as I encourage each of you to live with serenity the years that the Lord has granted you, I feel a spontaneous desire to share fully with you my own feelings at this point of my life, after more than twenty years of ministry on the throne of Peter and as we await the arrival, now imminent, of the Third Millennium. Despite the limitations brought on by age, I continue to enjoy life. For this I thank the Lord. It is wonderful to be able to give oneself to the very end for the sake of the Kingdom of God!

At the same time, I find great peace in thinking of the time when the Lord will call me: from life to life! And so I often find myself saying, with no trace of melancholy, a prayer recited by priests after the celebration of the Eucharist: In hora mortis meae voca me, et jube me venire ad te—at the hour of my death, call me and bid me come to you. This is the prayer of Christian hope, which in no way detracts from the joy of the present, while entrusting the future to God's gracious and loving care.

18. "Iube me venire ad te!": this is the deepest yearning of the human heart, even in those who are not conscious of it.

Grant, O Lord of life, that we may be ever vividly aware of this and that we may savour every season of our lives as a gift filled with promise for the future.

Grant that we may lovingly accept your will, and place ourselves each day in your merciful hands.

And when the moment of our definitive "passage" comes, grant that we may face it with serenity, without regret for what we shall leave behind. For in meeting you, after having sought you for so long, we shall find once more every authentic good which we have known here on earth, in the company of all who have gone before us marked with the sign of faith and hope.

Mary, Mother of pilgrim humanity, pray for us "now and at the hour of our death". Keep us ever close to Jesus, your beloved Son and our brother, the Lord of life and glory.

Amen!

From the Vatican, 1 October 1999. —Karol Josef Wojtyla **(Pope John Paul II)**

Footnotes

1. SAINT JOHN DAMASCENE, *Exposition of the Orthodox Faith*, 2, 29.

2. Cf. *The Dignity of Older People and Their Mission in the Church and in the World*, Vatican City, 1998.

3. VIRGIL, "Fugit inreparabile tempus", *Georgics* III, 284.

4. Liturgy of the Easter Vigil.

5. SAINT IRENAEUS OF LYONS, *Adversus Haereses*, IV, 20, 4.

6. Cf. POPE JOHN PAUL II, Encyclical Letter *Centesimus Annus*, 18.

7. *Ibid.*, 23.

8. SAINT JOHN CHRYSOSTOM, *Commentary on the Letter to the Romans*, 9, 2.

9. 2 Cf. Cato Maior, seu *De Senectute*, 19, 70.

10. On "All is vanity and affliction of spirit", 5-6.

11. "Auget sapientiam, dat maturiora consilia": *Commentaria in Amos*, II, prol.

12. CORNEILLE, *Sertorius*, Act II, Scene 4, v. 717.

13. "Magna fuit quondam capitis reverentia cani": *Fasti*, V, 57.

14. *Sententiae*, XLII.

15. Cf. POPE JOHN PAUL II, Encyclical Letter *Evangelium Vitae*, 65.

16. Cf. *ibid.*

17. C.K. NORWID, "Nie tylko przyszlosc....", *Post Scriptum*, I, vv. 1-4.

18. "Levior fit senectus, eorum qui a iuventute coluntur et diliguntur", Cato Maior, seu *De Senectute*, 8, 26.

19. *Discourse upon Returning from the Country*, 11.

20. SECOND VATICAN ECUMENICAL COUNCIL, Pastoral Constitution on the Church in the Modern World, *Gaudium et Spes*, 18.

21. *Roman Missal*, Preface of Christian Death I.

22. *Ibid.*

23. Cf. SAINT FRANCIS OF ASSISI, *Canticle of the Creatures*.

24. *Letter to the Romans*, 7, 2.

(Editio Interneto da Libreria Editrice Vaticana)

AGEING WELL
IS
A
SELF-TAUGHT
ART

Life is not like a rehearsal for a stage play.

Life is real. Now.

What we think, now, and what we do, now, will directly affect the quality, and longevity of our lives.

Now, in maturity, we have choices which were not available to us in our infancy, when factors affecting the circumstances and psyche of our parents played their part in moulding our personalities. But, having said that, it is clear beyond doubt that every one of us is blissfully, maddeningly, charmingly, frustratingly, animatedly, idiosyncratically—unique.

Who were these parents who established our individuality? Were they affluent, or needy? Healthy, or infirm? What were the hereditary traits, mingled in the cauldron of our parent's love, which were passed on to us in our genetic makeup?

To what extent did our parent's behaviour and spiritual affiliations affect our relationships with the other kids on the block?

Did our parents subscribe to beliefs which were recognizably admirable to us, and capable of being mirrored with enthusiasm—or were we rebels on a search for other causes which were hard to identify?

Were our parents good role models? Did they ever read Cicero? Or, were they the rebels, grappling with the shortcomings in their own lives? Were we the ones who grew up wanting to conform with normal societal backgrounds?

In our familial environment, what was the batting order? Were we first, or last, to get our feet into the sustenance trough? Or suffocating in the middle, under the acquisitiveness of boisterous siblings?

Most of us acquire our adult characteristics by a process of reaction to our environments during our developing years. This process of subconscious, and often imperfect, adaptation produces interesting prototypes which, in many cases, become raisons d'etre for well meaning shrinks.

Some years ago, I questioned the inevitability of growth through circumstance and engaged in a mind play which seems to be bearing fruit. I wonder if it could help to improve your own life?

The concept is simple. First, we form a picture of the world in which we live. In that world we create a mental picture of a person. You. All we are concerned with is you.

That's a simple idea. We are what we are.

Outside our earthly domain there is a deity. A god, or goddess. A supernatural, divine being. A Mahatma. Buddha. Jehovah. Lord of Lords. The all seeing one. The man upstairs.

The man upstairs, looking down at us, knows everything and everyone.

He knows exactly why he put us on this earth, and what he equipped us to do, to maximize his expectations of our fulfillment and happiness.

The only problem—and it's a real problem for many people—is that he didn't tell us what he had in mind when he put us here.

Now, ask yourself this question. "Would it have made any difference to my life, if I had known from my very early days, what god put me on this earth to do?"

Would it have been helpful to us, in kindergarten, if we'd been given the formula for maximizing our potential, because it is clear beyond doubt that getting started early on the real journey of life has produced some extraordinary results.

For example: Johan Sebastian Bach, Ludwig van Beethoven, Frederic Chopin, Galileo, Gary Kasparov, Genghis Khan, Yehudi Menuhin, Michelangelo, Wolfgang Amadeus Mozart, Isaac Newton, Pablo Picasso, Leonard da Vinci.

Tiger Woods.

Every one of these infant prodigies knew at an early age what god put them on this earth to do. Not having that advantage ourselves, and probably not being geniuses, what are the lessons we can learn which might brighten our days?

Asking ourselves the fundamental question could be a good start.

"What did god put me on this earth to do?"

Have you ever asked yourself that question?

"What did god put me on this earth to do?"

Are you doing it?

Did he really intend you to be sitting in front of a computer for eight hours a day?

Or spending two hours a day in a train, a car or a bus, traveling to and from a job you don't enjoy?

Or standing in a production line, performing a task which would create boredom in an unambitious chimpanzee?

Helping an irate customer crush her size seven feet into size five shoes?

Telling a sick patient that smoking forty gaspers a day will not improve one's life expectancy?

Swearing on your mother's grave that this stock you're selling will double in value over the next six months?

Is that it? What's it all about, Alfie?

A large number of people would say they're doing their boring job—for the money. I'm sure that's true, but what exactly should be the purpose of earning the money?

Surely, god didn't put us here to suffer the crucifixion of boredom or to make us the richest person in the graveyard.

A large number of people would say they accumulate their fortune to provide security for their families after they've gone to their bunkhouse in the sky. They keep their tabs on the loot until they fall off the perch in their eighties, and then, after the tax man has put his shovel in the pile, the elderly, long suffering successors are left to work out the logistics of the next stage in their journey.

With luck, this scenario gets short circuited by the early discovery of our true purpose in life, and we don't spend our time waiting for someone else to endow us with riches.

"What did god put me on this earth to do?"

Let's get some fun into this treatise on experiential thought, and see if we can find a clue or two about prospects for fulfillment. Let's see what the popular songwriters have said about getting it together.

All You Need Is The Air That You Breathe
(You can last a lot longer without food and water than you can without oxygen. Are you really concentrating on your breathing?)

I Will Always Love You
(Loving someone passionately is almost as good as loving yourself. Passionately.)

It's Now Or Never
(Life is not a rehearsal. Start today. Go for it.)

She Loves You
(Even better if you love each other.)

Whatever Will Be Will Be
(If you believe that, you'll believe anything. Make up your mind what you want and go for it.)

Release Me
(From the misery of continuing to do what I've always done when I know I'd be happier and more fulfilled doing something else.)

The Power of Love

(Is the ultimate power. It will enable you to move mountains.)

I Want To Hold Your Hand
(Because one plus one makes three. You both get something extra when you really love someone.)

You'll Never Walk Alone
(But you can walk alone, without fear, if you know where you want to go.)

Imagine
(Creating your own world, exactly the way you want it to be.)

I Owe You Nothing
(You've paid your dues. Now start living for today—your way.)

Make It Easy On Yourself
(You're the best person to make it easy on yourself, because you know exactly what you're missing.)

I Have A Dream
(If you have a dream—live your dream. Now.)

Beg, Steal or Borrow
(Beg, steal or borrow the only thing which is worth a damn—your personal freedom.)

Nineteenth Nervous Breakdowns
(Show me a liberated person and I'll show you a person who isn't going to have a breakdown.)

You Can Get It If You Really Want
(That's all you need to know. Do you really want it?)

The Best Things In Life Are Free
(And the very best thing is love. You and them.)

You Make Me Feel Like Dancing
(Now you're getting the idea!)

Don't Throw Your Love Away
(Cherish it. Today. Now.)

Good Vibrations
(Can you feel it!)

All You Need Is Love
(That is the absolute truth, and loving yourself is the absolute, absolute truth.)

I'd like to share with you, the words to a song I wrote some time ago.

Every evening star
Is a life at rest
Looking down at us
Fussing and fighting
Spirits in the sky
Know the reason why
We can carry on
Making our hopeful journey

Love is the reason
Why the world will survive
Life fades away
Then starts again
All through the changes
There's a new dream for us
And why
Love is the reason why

Every baby's cry
Is a miracle
We are born again
Life is beginning
Love will find the way
It's another day
It's another heart
Starting another story.

Are you ready?

Go.

—John Timperley

CREATIVITY
KNOWS
NO
AGE

Time: The Present

Place: An East Side Townhouse in Manhattan, New York City, USA

Characters: A Painter, Rudi, and a Performing Artist, Wynne

Wynne: As practitioners in the worlds of Fine Art and the Performing Arts we can testify to the truth that creativity knows no age because each working day has always led us on a quest for excellence which is greater than that which went before. There is a constant reappraisal of concept, technique, discipline and the ability to deal with other people who are crucial to the project. This has nothing to do with age. I have found that in reviewing my professional life, I have been engaged in both singing and acting from a very young age, either alone, or with others. It has always been a great joy to me to feel that with each professional challenge, I have taken knowledge gained from past experience and used it to enhance and improve whatever the current project might be.

I began my life as a musician. I come from a musical family. My mother was a pianist-organist and my father a trumpet player and conductor. I started piano lessons at an early age and then became a clarinetist playing with the Philharmonic in my hometown, Greeley, Colorado. This kind of experience proved invaluable for disciplined musicianship. When I reached the appropriate age, I began singing lessons and performed my first professional engagement as a singer while I was in high school.

When I left home I moved to San Francisco where I participated in the very active musical life of that great city. I sang as a soloist with the San Francisco Symphony, concertized extensively and entered the field of radio and TV with my own TV show for Sherman Clay Music Company and a radio show for KNBC. I also entered the glorious World of "Lieder"—art songs from around the world. It was pointed out to me by my coach, Lawrence Strauss, that I have a real God-given talent for projecting the "inner meaning" of songs to the audience. His way of saying it was that one must approach the song from "within out". What were your early experiences in the "fine art" world?

Rudi: I was born in Salzburg, Austria. I was surrounded from birth by the elegant architecture, artistic and musical sensibilities of my native city and by the surrounding mountains and countryside. My interest in portraits began at the age of ten when I was posing for a woman artist who was painting me in the pastel medium. This experience piqued my interest in the possibility of my becoming a portrait painter. At a very early age my parents took me to Vienna to enhance my appreciation of the arts. When I saw Schonbrunn, the magnificent Hapsburg Summer Palace, in its splendor, I immediately asked to be allowed to return the next day to paint this extraordinary landscape. I have since been told that this painting was truly remarkable for a nine year old. I believe that this painting encouraged my parents to enroll me for study at the Kunstler Haus in Salzburg where I began my basic instructions and learned discipline in an academic way. Copying Albrecht Durer drawings was part of the "ABCs" of my education among other things. But all that academic work changed in later years when I attended the L'Ecole de Beaux Arts in Paris. There I began to appreciate the French Impressionists which proved to be the influence for the rest of my painting days.

Wynne: I arrived in New York, as many young hopefuls do, to make my mark in the performing arts world! As I began to make contacts everyone said, 'You belong in musical comedy!' This meant learning an entirely new set of skills called acting! Fortunately I was sent to the studio of Betty Cashman in the Carnegie Hall building. I say fortunate because Betty taught the British technique of acting, snap your finger and you are in the character you wish to portray and snap your finger and you are out of character and restored to your real self. This avoided all of the damaging psychological effects of the Actors Studio which was so prominent at that time. The Cashman method included voice work, pronunciation and enunciation drills as well as "scene work". All of the work was designed to free one from inhibitions about performing one's inmost thoughts as the character, and at times I felt as though I were walking across the Grand Canyon on a tight rope. Betty also taught the different acting techniques for performing in theatre, television and film. I have been very fortunate to have worked in all these mediums as well as concert and cabaret. I have also lectured extensively on Glenn Miller who was my uncle.

I also found myself learning a great deal about dealing with people. This was required by the "Cashman Technique". In the performing arts one is constantly interacting with other actors, singers, musicians, technical crew, directors, conductors, makeup people, etc. A wise attitude in dealing with these fellow workers is an absolute necessity. O, did I forget agents and managers?

I must have learned my lessons well because I soon found myself making my Broadway debut as Daisy Mae in "Lil Abner" for which I won a "Theatre World Award". "Thurber Carnival" quickly followed and "Tenderloin" with George Abbott directing and Maurice Evans starring. From there I went into television with a daytime drama, "Somerset," for NBC and appearances on the Tonight Show and Today Show as well as many other TV appearances, including commercials, too numerous to mention. This phase of my professional life taught me what I know at this point to be an absolute truth—that no matter where we are on life's highway we are always growing. And at this mature age, where I find myself, I feel that this creative urge is stronger than ever.

Rudi: I came to the Untied States on a visitor's visa and when the time ran out I returned to Austria not realizing that Hitler's Anschluss had already taken place. My family urged me to return quickly to America, and fortunately I was able to escape back to the United States, but I was again forced to leave the country. I went to Mexico for six months and, at the end of that time, I became an American citizen. I served in the American Army in World War II. My basic training was with the Combat Engineers but I was later transferred to The Recruiting Publicity Bureau, U.S. Army. I created many recruiting posters including 'Army Nurses Needed Now' which hangs in the Surgeon General's Office in Washington, D.C. Many of my posters were seen on billboards nationwide. At the end of my army career I studied with Dimitri Romanovsky, a pupil of William Chase and Robert Henri. As fate would have it I was fortunate to occupy the studio of Robert Henri in the Lincoln Arcade Building which stood where Lincoln Center is now. Wynne, as you mentioned when you came to New York you had a life changing experience and I felt exactly the same way; of course, I was an immigrant living an entirely new life style in the "New World" during very precarious times. But still I felt that creative urge to keep painting. Fortunately, I was able to fulfill this dream painting generals and admirals in my army years. How have you fulfilled this "creative urge" in your later years in New York?

Wynne: I have returned to the cabaret-concert world appearing here in New York in two different cabarets, "Wynne Miller Sings Glenn Miller", and "To Glenn With Love" at the Algonquin Hotel. I have also recorded a new CD, "Winners", for Emerald Records in Nashville as well as recordings in Europe for Union Music of Austria. I have been inducted into the Big Band Hall of Fame in Palm Beach, Florida and also lectured for the Cunard Line on the QEII and Coronia about my uncle, Glenn Miller, whose 100th birthday was celebrated worldwide on March 1, 2004. I appeared at many theatrical clubs here in New York and throughout the United States to honor him and to celebrate Glenn's recognition as a great musician and true patriot who gave his life for his country in World War II. I have found just recently, thanks to life long urging by the Creative Power, that a clearer understanding of proper vocal technique has been revealed to me after a life long study. Hooray for maturity! Another avenue of creative expression has opened to me which has been quite surprising—that of writing. I enjoy it and opportunities to do so seem to open unexpectedly. One never knows where the creative urge will strike!

Rudi: One of my famous sitters was Fritz Kreisler, the world renowned violinist, who was good friend and fellow Austrian. The two portraits I did of him are the only portraits in existence and Fritz left them in my care. They were returned to the Musikverein in Vienna where he graduated at the age of ten, a Wunderkind extraordinaire.

Later I moved my studio to the upper floor of my brownstone on the upper east side of Manhattan which serves as my artistic sanctuary to this very day. I find that my sitters are very happy there listening to the carriages from Central Park returning to the barn with their "clip clop, clip clop" which carries us all to a former century. I have learned that playing music is a great part of a successful portrait. I have found that one paints with colors as a conductor conducts an orchestra. Some things are brought forward; others are pushed into the background. Some colors are intensified while others are subdued—just the way a conductor would lead his orchestra. It all starts with the composition of the sitter and that is part of the relationship between music and art. Of course, with each portrait, landscape, nude, still life or flower painting, I advance my knowledge and I am reminded of the Old Russian saying of my mentor, Dimitri Romanovsky, "Learn a lifetime, die a fool!"

Wynne: Who are some of the people you have painted and were they all painted in your studio?

Rudi: Many too numerous to mention were painted "on location", as you would say in show business, Wynne. The Emir of Kuwait, Ernest and Jack Hemingway, Princess Agathe Schonburg-Hartenstein of Austria, the Prince Archbishop of Salzburg, General MacArthur, Gary Cooper, military people, society people, politicians, clergymen, theatrical people, etc., etc. Or, as I always say, "I have painted everyone from Gypsy Rose Lee to Cardinal Spellman." And so, Wynne, philo-sophically speaking, how do you think this maturity we have so unexpectedly reached has affected your performing abilities?

Wynne: I find that I have acquired a much broader understanding of the disci-plines involved in my profession. I have lived longer and therefore life's experi-ences have given me a much broader understanding of the human condition which I am charged with conveying to an audience. This becomes a great advan-tage as an actress. One can delve into one's own life experiences as well as the observations one has of the life experiences of others for unlimited materials; they add breadth and scope to one's portrayals which were not even dreamed of in younger years. I find my self "accentuating the positive", the happy side of life, much more now that in former times. What about you, Rudi? What help do you find with your "new found" maturity?

Rudi: Pretty much of what you have just mentioned seems to apply to me. I now have a much greater assurance that the painting I am creating, with the accumu-lation of knowledge achieved through all these years, whether it be a portrait or another type of painting, will meet my exacting standards. Of course portraits are the most demanding because one must create not just a likeness, but a painting worthy of being called "fine art!" This is where the years of knowledge and expe-rience come into play. This knowledge and experience is also invaluable when dealing with the personalities involved in portrait painting. Diplomacy is the order of the day.

Wynne: I too, have found that diplomacy in dealing with the myriad personali-ties involved in the performing arts has become much easier as maturity has arrived. One has much more tolerance and understanding toward one's cowork-ers. There are times, also, when one can actually help younger performers. One can also demand that certain professional standards must be accepted for the actual physical protection of all involved. I must say, though, that my impatience with poorly trained, incompetent coworkers has remained to this day—or possi-bly increased.

Rudi: Another aspect of growth might be that one feels so much more secure hav-ing achieved success and gone through the growing pains of youthful endeavor. To work from experience gives one the freedom to concentrate totally on the project at hand. This would include being able to handle location and different environmental situations, with sometime difficult lighting conditions and away from my familiar studio light. This would also include not having the proper equipment at hand, such as a model stand and an easel and having to improvise on the job.

Wynne: I know what you mean. I was trained to project the voice to the top row of the balcony WITHOUT microphones! Nowadays, if a "mike" fails, I don't panic—I project! What a comfort it is to know that one has the technique to do that. This all comes with the accumulation of years of experience.

Rudi: Yes, in my case I never know who the next sitter will be—what their personality will be—how many times they will be able to pose for me—or how the result of my painting will be seen by the family of the sitter. I remember a distinguished member of a great literary family, who, at my request, selected his own wardrobe. He had chosen a beautiful dark green velvet dinner jacket with black satin lapels. He was most pleased with my work. Then his wife appeared on the scene and rejected the whole painting. I suspected that she wanted him to look like a combination of Tyrone Power and John Wayne dressed in cowboy gear! So you never know. Fortunately, this was the only such case in the hundreds of portraits I have painted. This would have been a devastating experience in my younger years, but in maturity it was just an annoyance from an immature person. In contrast to this case, I remember so clearly a posthumous portrait I painted of a university president. When his wife came to view it she burst into tears saying "you have brought my husband back to life!"

Wynne: It seems to me, Rudi, that you have always loved your art and have had a very mature outlook on it which has not changed that much over the years.

Rudi: You are absolutely right. From what you have told me, Wynne, you feel much differently about your growth process. Could you explain that?

Wynne: I feel that my maturity has come the hard way as a person, and that my lifelong involvement in the arts has helped me to reach a state of maturity which I had not thought possible. Now I enjoy life and performing so much more than in my early years when I was acquiring all the technical experience needed for professional work. I feel so grateful to still be performing and really gain tremendous satisfaction from bringing music, beauty and amusement to an audience. I love comedy and have always been involved in lighter, comedic material. I believe that my profession is a worthy soul endeavor and it is fun—much more fun than in the earlier years.

Rudi: I concur. In later years, painting has become more enjoyable and satisfying for me also. My studio is my inner sanctum and there is no other place on earth I would rather be. And so, Wynne, after much discussion, I believe we have come to a mutual agreement that as one advances in years, we find ourselves constantly improving in technique, appreciation, creativity and, especially, in understanding our chosen art forms. There seems to be no end to the knowledge for which one is reaching and that would lead one to conclude there is a powerful Creative Force in the universe which supplies unlimited ideas on demand. Cicero would agree with us: MATURITY COMES BY LEARNING—NOT BY AGE.

—Wynne Miller

—Rudolf Anton Bernatschke

Enjoying the Autumn of Life

Accept the Ageing Process with the Right Attitude

With age, we face new experiences that never appeared during our youth or middle age. If these problems cannot be treated in a right way, they will cause personal problems; they will then reduce the quality of life and accelerate the ageing process. These problems are expressed in many aspects. I have experienced the following ten:

1. Energy. When one is young, he/she may be a master when working. He/she may be powerful and outstanding in nearly every field. When he/she enters into the aged stage, he/she would like to continue these abilities. One always wants to compete with youngsters, but sometimes we are not equal to our ambition. So they feel disappointed and retreat in defeat. Such examples occur commonly. Therefore, the aged must have the right self-awareness. They must learn to admit to "value reduction". Just do things that are appropriate to one's age. Act according to one's abilities and stop when one should stop. Only through this way can it be helpful to keep a balanced mind and a healthy body.

2. Adapt to be on the fringe of crowd. When you are young, perhaps you are the main force of your unit. You are the center of your unit and there are always so many people surrounding you. But now you become aged and retired, you are on the fringe of society, being sometimes listed in the disadvantaged group of people who need support. It is a natural fact, a natural social phenomenon. Don't be depressed. Just accept change calmly and face it positively.

3. Who is master? In traditional Chinese families, the elder is the center. The more senior one becomes, the more respect he receives. The paterfamilias decides all matters. Such a tradition changes with the emerging market economy. The order of the noble and the humble and the order of the senior and the junior have been shattered and placed upside down. At present, there are a majority of one-child families in China. In such a 4-2-1 structured family (4 patrilineal grandparents and matrilineal grandparents; 2 parents; 1 child), the child is the most favorite object. He/she is the so-called "little emperor" while the senior (especially the grandparents) are all on the fringe of the family, perhaps even in a subordinate position. It is an unreasonable but a widespread phenomenon. On the one hand, filial piety still needs to be advocated in society. The seniors should educate the child to be filial to his/her parents,

to respect seniority, and to carry forward such traditional Chinese values. On the other hand, when the elderly are educating their children to obey the filial standard they do not have to care who is the master. The elderly should positively adjust to the new family structure so as to keep a pleasant mood.

4. Change. With the development of China's open and reform policy, a huge change has taken place, in housing and decoration to clothes, in eating and drinking to hairstyles, and in language and culture. The changes are rather quick and dazzling. Some aged people dislike some changes and sigh with regret that "today is worse than before" and denounce the changes as deteriorating morals and manners. And some will become very angry and depressed once they see such changes. My view is just let it be. Firstly, from the comprehensive perspective, one can understand that such changes are good and that society has diversified and become prosperous. It is a symbol of social progress. The elderly should welcome them. Also it would be better for them to choose appropriate projects to participate in and share in the happiness of modern fashion. Secondly, to be frank, sometimes bad things do occur. I believe that they will be eliminated during the development of a more spiritual civilization, a process of supporting the good and eliminating the bad. So the elderly need not worry about it.

5. Old is beautiful. Some aged people do not want to go out nor make friends. Why? They feel they are so old and ugly that they do not want to be seen any more. It is a biased view. It is undeniable that when a man becomes old, wrinkles will appear on the face, the hair will fall out and even his back may become crooked. However, it is a natural phenomenon. It doesn't mean that the elderly cannot meet others any more. On the contrary, aged people should pay more attention to their appearance and to their temperaments. There is an old saying: "One will be of considerable talent if he/she has done a great deal of reading; and one will be naturally noble if he/she has no dissatisfaction". Let's take dressing for example. One should like dressing a lot more as he/she becomes older. Nice dressing not only pleases another's eyes, but also can make him/her happy. This is because nice dressing can change the state of mind of the elderly. The elderly can then reach a realm of elegance and confidence through aesthetic taste and self-improvement. Once their state of mind becomes peaceful, their mood will naturally become better. The experts specialized in the aged people's health think that one should never discount the importance of dressing well. The brain will become more active and the ageing process will be delayed when one is striving to beautify

himself/herself. A survey recently carried out, with more than 3,000 people, has proven that those who care for their appearance suffer less than 30% of psychologically relevant diseases (including hypertension) than those who do not care.

6. Exercise by walking. Some aged people feel that their legs and feet do not work well and they have to walk slowly. So they do not want to walk, let alone going far way from home. But the result is if one doesn't move he will not want to move at all. Finally, he/she cannot walk. Thus a vicious circle. How to solve it? The key is to change the concept. One should stick to exercise because his/her legs and feet are becoming older. According to many aged people, walking half an hour everyday (some people walk for an hour), rather than riding, can keep the legs and feet agile. People sometimes say "contemptible bone" which means that the bone likes exercise rather than rest. If you allow it to rest, it will become lazy and thus become useless quickly. Encourage each other: "Let's go for a walk." Walking will bring health and beauty; walking will lead us into a new world.

7. Memory Matters. Some aged people think they are old and the memory must become poor. So they do not want to remember anything at all and always ask others to remember for them. In fact, the brain will work better if it is often used. Not strengthening thinking is one of the causes of dementia for aged people. According to my experience, the ways to improve memory capability (or delay the memory's ageing process) are as follows:

    a. Foster the habit of remembering: You can start by remembering something you are interested in, such as poetry, rhymes, etc.

    b. Use tricks to remember something vital but hard to remember (such as a theory or a formulation). Then you can strengthen your memory and remember the things well.

    c. In order to strengthen your memory, you can read aloud and with your friends.

    d. Keep a notebook and review it in order to help the memory.

8. Reduction of income. Some aged people are not satisfied with retirement income that is less than before. In fact, it should be treated in a right way. There are two reasons: Firstly, you have become older. You are not a major force in production (or work) any longer. Furthermore, a lot of young peo-

ple are waiting to be employed and jobs are limited. All of the countries worldwide are adopting the same measures. Secondly, when you retire, expenditures will decrease a lot. Just be ready to accept such change and make a sound expenditure budget. I believe you can live a good life this way.

9. Loneliness. When he/she is still working in the unit, he/she can enjoy many events due to versatile intercourse. But when he/she retires, the environment changes and social contacts become fewer. So he/she may feel lonely. One should be ready to address loneliness. He/she must then communicate more with his/her family members, relatives and friends, especially with those old friends who have similar situations. They can meet and be as lively and active as before. Learn to look forward. Never look backward.[1]

10. Bad Temper. I divide the aged people I have seen into two categories. As for the first type, the older they become, the more the temper. They are very easily angry, always wanting to quarrel with someone. They were called "dotard" or "old devil's advocates". As for as the second type, the older they become, the more tolerant they become. They become more peaceful and always ready to listen to others' advice. Confucius called them "A sixty-year old man with a clever ear". They are those people call "wise elders" or "kind elders". It goes without saying that all aged people should learn from the second type. They should be the popular and venerable elder people. But people should show enough care and consideration to the first type of people also. Proper measures should be taken to persuade them to be even-tempered and good humored so as to help them to get along with people. This will be beneficial to both sides. And of course this will be helpful to improving their health.

Countermeasures against Ageing

Although people cannot resist and reverse the ageing process, people can delay it and improve their life quality in older years. According to the biological theory, the lifespan of mammals is 5-7 times their growth period. The growth period of a human is projected that, on the basis of the time that the last tooth comes out (e.g. 20-25 years old), the shortest lifespan of human should be 100-years, and the longest should be 175-years. It is acknowledged that the normal lifespan of human should be 120-years old.[2]

The World Health Organization (WHO) has mentioned some points: There are four elements that constitute human's longevity, in which the heredity from parents accounts for 15%, social and natural environment account for 10% and 7% respectively (altogether 17%), a medical condition accounts for 8% and individual lifestyle accounts for 60%. It can be seen that a good lifestyle is the most important for delaying death and improving health conditions. Some recommendations follow:

1. Keep a balanced diet. The Victorian Proclamation developed three milestones for improving health conditions: Keep a balanced diet, do aerobic exercise and have a good state of mind. The prime factor is keeping a balanced diet. Drinking and eating are two different things. What is good for drinking? The answer is neither Coca-Cola nor Sprite. There are six kinds of health-friendly beverages recommended by the International Health Conference: The first one is green tea (containing tea-polyphenols which is an anticancer); the second one is red wine (there is revertase which wars is against senium); the third one is soybean milk; the fourth is yogurt; the fifth is bone soup (containing certain substances that can prolong life); and the sixth is mushroom soup. Although these things are good for drinking, the quantity you have must be appropriate. For example, you should not drink more red wine than 50-100 ml a day.

What is good for eating? A reasonable pyramid consists of three levels: grain, legumes and vegetables.

As for grain, corn comes into mind firstly (containing abundant lecithin, linoleic acid, grain alcohol, VE, etc.). The second one is buckwheat (which can reduce blood pressure, blood fat and blood sugar). And the third one is the potato family—white sweet potato, red sweet potato, yam and white potato (it can absorb moisture, fat and sugar, as well as toxins). As to legumes, beans contain a great deal of quality protein. In order to increase the quantity of quality protein in food, the China Health Ministry has developed a plan called "Soybean Activities Plan" which requires that everyone should ensure "a handful of vegetables, a handful of soybean, an egg and some meat" in their daily food.[3] Overeating and overdrinking these days has become the number one killer of people.

A recent study indicates that obesity caused by overeating and overdrinking will reduce the average lifespan of human by four or five years in the coming decades.

2. Sufficient sleep. Enough sleep everyday is vital for delaying ageing and improving life quality. There is a Chinese saying: "It would be better to have a long sleep rather than to have a pig one night".

WHO suggested five precautions to ensure good health: one should avoid colds, insomnia, fat, fatigue and anger. But how can one prevent insomnia? How can one improve sleep quality? WHO advanced several points to be noticed: Firstly, ensuring enough sleep time (generally 8 hours a day, it varies according to different people), especially the quality sleep time. Secondly, daily life must change according to the changing seasons. That is, getting up and going to bed early in spring; getting up early while going to bed late in summer and autumn, and going to bed early and getting up late in winter. Thirdly, maintain the right posture when sleeping. One should lie down on his/her right side in an arch-shape. Fourthly, the head should be on the north and the feet on the south, the same direction as the earth's magnetic field. Fifthly, there should remain as few as possible home appliances that make electromagnetic waves in the bedroom. Otherwise it will cause sleep disturbance. It is also surely helpful to soak your feet before sleeping.

3. Good state of mind. The ancients said, "It is the mind that creates the environment." One's happiness is created by one's mind. One's pain is also created by one's mind. Therefore, keeping a balanced state of mind is the key to preserving one's health.

In order to keep a balanced state of mind, the prime item is not to seek fame and wealth. Lao Tse said that "Happiness is less important than no worry, and wealth is less important than being content with one's lot." Happiness does not rely on how much one possesses. As far as I am concerned, there are five stages in a human's life: Natural life stage (from birth to youth); follower stage (imitate and follow others); vacillating life state (one begins to think for oneself as to where to go and how to go); self-conscious life stage (one has definite thought and marches along that road); and tasting life (one is living in the world while watching beyond the world and enjoying the taste of life). Entering the aged stage means you have entered the tasting life stage.

Neijing, one of the traditional Chinese medicine classical works, says "If the essence and the spirit are fixed in the body, how can one suffer diseases?" But how to keep the essence and spirit fixed in the body? According to a great herbalist doctor, firstly one should not overtax his/her spirit. Secondly, one should have the grace of cloud and water and the spirit of pine and cypress. That is, one should not be too depressed when in adversity and one should not be exultant or complacent when in favorable circumstances. Just as a saying in a couplet that a lot of celebrities believe: "Remain indifferent to other's opinion and look at the flowers blooming and withering with ease; having no intention to keep it or to let it leave and just look at those clouds on the horizon curling and extending." The famous traditional Chinese medical doctor Zhao Guang advocated that there are three ways to preserve health—taking pleasure in helping others, contentment and happiness and to be content with one's lot.

4. Exercise. Aerobic exercise works well for preventing disease and improving health. Scientific research indicates that it has the following main effects:

- Exercise can allow people to breath in oxygen several times more in average conditions;
- Exercise can reduce the fat in the body significantly;
- Exercise can improve one's mood and eliminate worry and trouble;
- Exercise can improve one's immune function;
- Exercise can expel poisonous elements in the body.

As to how to exercise, or when to exercise, or in what way to exercise and the amount of exercise, that depends on the individual. It should be adapted to the needs of each individual. Of course, over-exercising can cause harm and even lead to death. Therefore, just do an appropriate amount of exercise.

5. Divide work and rest. When entering into old age, one cannot work as hard or as long as a young person. Instead, one should learn to be relaxed and casual. It does not mean that one should be idle all day long. Even if one has retired from his/her original position, one should continue to look for some work to do. Rather than following rules docilely and only do routine work, one should seek some innovative work to do. One is expected to have initiative to face challenge, to find necessary stimulation. Of course this will help one's health. Health experts Chinese or foreign, think that the best way to keep the brain healthy is to provide continuous stimulus to it, that is, to give it new experiences. When certain new information enters into the brain, it will construct new connective loops to deal with it if there is no existing relevant network. In this way, it can boost the brain's growth and keep it healthy.

All kinds of work (including brainwork and manual work) contribute to one's metabolism. But one should pay attention to combine the work with rest. With increasing age, the elderly should work less and rest more. How much work or rest are the most appropriate? It depends on the condition of each individual. One should make adjustments according to one's own experience.

6. Do as many good deeds as possible. "The benevolent will live a long life" has been confirmed by most of the Chinese health experts through the ages. Confucius had developed that "morality benefits health" and "great kindness is certain to merit long life." "Benevolence" is defined as the sympathy and friendship between people. Shi Tianji, health expert of the Qing Dynasty, had written in his *Growth Secret*: "One who wants good health should make morality the main goal". Additionally, he developed six maxims to preserve good health: Always keep a peaceful mind; always be just; always be happy; always be merciful; always be kind and pleasant; and always preserve ease and comfort. Suppose that one is very kind and philanthropic and cares for others (especially the disadvantaged group of people) and serves society: on the one hand he/she will feel happy because he/she has devoted resources, wisdom and labor during this process; on the other hand, he/she will receive much more and much deeper love as a return because of such philanthropy. Thus one will be surrounded by love and feel the true warmth of the world. Thus a good circulation forms. The value of one's life will increase day by day. As a result, he/she will become much gentler and the objective of prolonging life is easily achieved.

7. Foster hobbies. When one becomes aged and retired, he/she will not do the work they did before now; they have time to develop their hobbies. It may be *qin*, chess, writing and painting, or it may be singing and dancing, or it may be cooking and baking, or it may be growing flowers and plants. As long as you love what you do and do it to a moderate degree, it will help to improve your health. Firstly, you will feel happy on the spiritual side when you develop your hobbies. Secondly, you will receive good exercise on the physical side. It will save you from ossification. Thirdly, during these activities you may meet many people who share a common interest with you. As a result, you can live a more interesting and amusing life. Lu You, a poet of the Song dynasty of China, has a unique insight concerning preserving health. He said growing flowers maintains a childlike innocence. His poems also give it a good expression: "It would be better for me to grow and appreciate the fragrant lily; in fact, such an aged man like me is still equipped with an innocent mind of a child". Research has shown that the volatile aroma oil in the petals and pistils have various pharmacological effects. To smell the flowers will be beneficial for improving health. At the same time, growing and appreciating flowers, not only can exercise one's bones and muscles but also can add flavor to life as well as cultivating one's sentiments.

8. Practice "chatting-therapy". People know that those who suffer cancers need chemotherapy. In fact, as for the health of aged people, "chatting-therapy" is more important. It is really necessary for each person. Humans have natural

attributes and the social attributes. Both the two attributes need communication with relatives and friends. If you speak happy things, others can share the happiness with you. But if you speak unhappy things, especially those painful ones, others will share with you and help you to find the key and resolve them. In this way you will feel you are suddenly enlightened. Here we have two points to note: Firstly, expand the "chatting-therapy" circle intentionally and make more friends. Secondly, you should initially seek these friends if you do have some problems. And when others have worries, you should listen to them carefully and help them to resolve them. It is never one-sided work (only speaking but not listening). The two aspects are interactive.

9. Get a regular health checkup. Professor Hong Zhao Guang's golden saying is that "the best medication is time". Generally speaking, one will recover if one takes timely treatment. On the contrary, if one does not get regular health checkups, he/she will have no knowledge that he/she is suffering the diseases (especially cancer). And when he knows it, it may be too late. Sometimes the disease develops, just because the patient makes a delay in treating it. It is a comprehensive checkup which can ensure any illnesses will be discovered in time.

10. Live in a natural way. Wang Chong, a philosopher in the Donghan Dynasty of China, has said (in *Lun Heng*) that growing naturally is the top priority for preserving health. People are different. Therefore, there may be no uniform way for preserving health for all people. Regarding diet, as long as one's spleen and stomach work well, the food one takes will be normally digested, absorbed and excreted. There is no need to worry that taking food will bring disease. Contrarily, being hungry but not eating will lead to a poor nutrition supply and decreasing Qi and blood. It will ultimately do harm to health, even lead to unexpected harm in the long run. As for exercise and good health, it is also based on the individual. Do not imitate others painstakingly. Do not copy mechanically regardless of specific conditions.

The ten aspects mentioned above interact with each other. If you want to reap the fruit of a long life, the most important thing is perseverance. Never work by fits and starts. Never leave something half done. The philosophy for preserving health, from knowing when to take action, then taking action to continuous action, needs firm belief as well as strong willpower. Whether you can live up to it is also a test for the character of a person. Some experts outline the philosophy of good health as "insistence is its base, appropriation is its core, details are its key and balance is its root".[4]

The Nature of Ageing

Everything on earth experiences birth, growing and ageing. It is the natural way of life. The human being is of no exception. The year can be divided into spring, summer, autumn and winter and the stages of the human being can be classified into childhood, youth, prime of life and the aged period. Freedom only comes when one accepts the certainty. If people do, they will live life in a natural way. Then they can face the ageing process calmly and, thus have a happy and comfortable old age.

Scientists have found there are 10 major reasons contributing to the ageing process.

1. Chronic inflammation: With increasing age, the organs of the body will experience more and more inflammations, such as arthritis. The parts that suffer are not only joints, but also brain cells, artery walls and valves. Stroke has also to do with inflammation.

2. Gene mutation: Many natural and man-made factors can cause gene mutation. With increasing age, the cells' processing mechanism becomes more and more irregular, thus leading to genetic retrogression and deterioration.

3. Exhaustion of cells' energy: The cells' "power plant"—mitochondrion—needs certain chemical materials to ensure the cells' vigor and to clear away the toxin hidden in the cells. If the "charging" process becomes weakened, the musculature decay, chronic fatigue and neuropathic disease can develop.

4. Imbalance among hormones: The hormones make hundreds of millions cells in our bodies work synchronously and precisely. If the balance is broken up, various diseases will happen, including depression, osteoporosis and coronary arteriosclerosis.

5. Calcifying effect: The Ca ion passes in and out of the cell through special channels in the cell membrane. Once one becomes decrepit, the channels for Ca ion to pass in and out are then deteriorated, resulting in an overabundance of Ca remaining in the brain cell, valves and blood vessel walls.

6. Imbalance among the fatty acids: The body needs fatty acids to produce the energy needed. The older one becomes, the more enzyme deficiency

occurs. Consequently, one will experience arhythmia, joint decay, or may be subjected to fatigue or dry skin.

7. Imbalance among non-digestive enzymes: Many kinds of enzyme reaction are taking place synchronously in the cells. But such balance becomes weaker year by year. It firstly happens in the brain and liver. That is the reason why neuropathic disease and toxicosis tissue trauma have been caused.

8. Lack of digestive enzyme: The pancreas becomes exhausted little by little so that it cannot produce enough enzymes. As a result, the digestive system loses some of its chronic mechanism.

9. Exhaustion of blood circulation: The capillary vessels will suffer after many years of functioning, including those in the brain, eyes and skin. As a result, a stroke (major or minor) will occur, the eyesight will decline, and wrinkles will appear.

10. Oxidation irritated responsiveness: Free radicals can cause a lot of trouble for people at any age will bring more trouble for middle-aged people. They can affect the natural physiological development, thus increasing the burden of the body and results in various diseases.[5]

That an aged person should face the ageing process calmly is not only because it is irreversible, but also because it is a self-conscious eco-ethical pursuit with no alternative. The resources supporting human being on earth are limited and it is said the earth's ultimate capacity is six billion people. If this ageing generation did not disappear, it would have to struggle with their descendants for available resource and space. But the young people and the middle-aged people are the main force who are creating wealth for humanity and contributing to social development. In China they also have to provide for the comfort of the aged people who have lost the ability to work. If the proportion of the two factors becomes imbalanced little by little, the proportion of aged people becomes too large and the dependents outweigh independents, then society will develop at a slow speed. It surely will lead to certain negative effects. Therefore, as a man having experienced great changes in the world, a man having a sense of responsibility and mission, he will neither be antipathetic nor refuse this progress when facing the natural ageing phenomenon. Contrarily, he/she will treat it in a positive and optimistic manner. It is said that when Lao Tse's wife died, he congratulated her on her death by playing a musical instrument rather than crying. Maybe he knew the truth.

The Setting Sun is Equally Splendid

There is an old but famous saying that describes the conditions of aged people. "The setting sun is definitely nice, but it is really a pity that it is near dusk". However, the modern famous saying in China is "Why bother to regret that the setting sun is drawing near dusk as long as it is definitely nice?" I hold the same view as the latter one. Besides, it is just some artistic description to describe the ageing stage as "dusk". Perhaps it is not precise when we view it from the scientific perspective.

"The setting sun is definitely nice." Why?

Let's take a comprehensive look. According to WHO standards, aged people can be divided into three groups: Younger elder—from 65 to 74; elder—from 75 to 89; long-life elder—over 90. When life goes into its ageing stage, it is not a process toward withering, failing and loneliness. Instead, it is a process that people are integrating, summarizing and reviewing things on a high-level. And it is a harvest season when aged people should re-create brilliance.

In this harvest season, there are heaps of fruits that you have made painstaking effort to grow all your life and now are coming to you: The children have grown with talent; you have made a lot of friends; you have taught many students who are scattered in every corner of the world (if you are a teacher); you have written many great works (if you are a scholar);—and you perhaps have more important fruits to gather (except for wealth).

When you are old, you possess half a century or more of extensive experience. Based on this, you can summarize and integrate your life so as to build a grander mansion. Maybe it is industry or business. Maybe it is discoveries or inventions. Maybe it is some books or writings. Of course, it may be new knowledge or skills or arts. Or maybe, travel together with friends or perform on the stage to realize the dreams that started in younger years.

Great minds mature slowly; a good sword never gets dull. Research has been developed at Kentucky University in the United States on the relation between aged people and early ageing dementia, tracking the health status of 678 over-70 years old Catholic nuns. The eldest one is Esther Bull who is 107 years old now. She has been interested in ceramics since she retired at 97 years old. Since then she has been so creative that at last she became a famous artist.

Professor Fei Xiatong, who passed away on April 24, 2005, is the founder of China's modern sociology and anthropology. He has devoted all his life to teaching and research. His creativity and scientific achievements reached the highest point when he was old. He never ceased researching or teaching until his death at

95 years old. Based on a great deal of cases, the researchers have found that old age can become the most fruitful period for creativity. There is a scientific foundation for it. That is, the brain of a healthy adult contains about 100 billion nerve cells, some of which die with the increase of the age. However, the other parts of the brain are also growing at the same time as long as it can get enough stimuli. Dr. James Kern, director of the Health Research Center of Washington University in the United States, concluded: "The dendrite will grow in the brain cell with the passing of time, especially when one is challenged". From more than 50 years old to more than 70 years old, substantial dendrite will grow in the information processing area of the brain.

Scientists are trying to find the secret that keeps the brain active. Professor Marrian Damond, comprehensive biology professor at the University of California at Berkeley in the United States, has listed five factors: diet, exercise, challenge, curiosity and care. It is obvious that nutrition is of great importance. Exercise is equally important to the cardiovascular and the respiratory system that keep the brain active. Experience has proved that if the rats used for experiment have a new maze or various toys with which to play, their brains will become more sophisticated and penetrating. If the scientists give them continuous stimulus, their lives will be extended from 600 days to 900 days.[6]

Therefore, it depends on a person's state of mind whether or not he/she can enjoy the happiness of the harvest period and whether or not he/she can re-create and maintain brilliance when they become old. Cicero proposed the same viewpoint 2100 years ago when he wrote in his book *On Old Age*: "Do all you can to develop the study and practice of decent, enlightened living and as life draws to a close the harvest you reap will be amazing. That is partly for the very important reason that you can go on living in this fashion until your dying day. Besides, there is great satisfaction in the knowledge of a life well spent and the memory of many things well done." (Bk 1) Dismiss the stereotyped concept of "the old must be slow-witted". Learn to preserve health scientifically. Stick to exercise. Dare to face continuous challenges. Dominate your life. In this way, "the setting sun" is surely to glitter and turn a new page.

A happy and brilliant old age does not happen by chance; rather; it is the result of continuous effort and creativity.

—Cao Qingyang

Footnotes

1. Yin Bo, "*Enjoying Dressing up Is Helpful to Keep Health*, from *Chinese Aged People,*" Nov. 1 2005.

2. From Professor Hong Shaoguang's lecture on health, held in Zhongnanhai, Beijing, 2004.

3. See also *Professor* Qi <u>Guoli</u> *Talking About Health*

4. Zu Guansheng, "The Details of Life Determine the Lifespan," included in *Wen Wei PO Daily*, Shanghai, April 20, 2005.

5. Ding Yongming, "Scientists' Proposition: 10 Major Factors for Aging," included in *Health and Life*, February 21, 2005.

6. Callen S. Seibert, "Become Old Artistically," *Newsweek* , Mar. 6, 2005.

Biographic Digests of Contributing Authors

✦

(Listed according to their article's appearance in the text)

Richard Jones, born in Wales, was the BBC and Reuters correspondent in Beirut when he began writing popular novels, such as *The Age of Wonder* and *Supper With the Borgias*. Later he served as Professor of Creative Writing at The University of Virginia, The University of Charleston and Lynchburg College in the United States.

Peter Abbey, named for the famous 18th Century French cleric, soldier, scholar, romantic, writer and abbot, resides in Monaco and claims to have endeavored to live up to his famed ancestor's standards with his many books and his varied articles on current and classical cultures.

William A. Johnson served both Brandeis University as the Albert V. Danielson Professor of Philosophy and Christian Thought and the Cathedral Church of Saint John the Divine in New York as its Canon Theologian.
Porfessor Johnson teaches annually in Australia, Denmark and the USA.

Josef Kolenski was born in Philadelphia, Pennsylvania (USA) of Polish Russian immigrant parents and at 17 became a Hinayana Buddhist. He is a practicing psychiatrist by profession and a painter by preference.

Ralph N. Wharton is Clinical Professor of Psychiatry at Columbia University Medical Center in New York and the author of many notable articles and papers as well as co-author of the recent *Textbook of Neurology*.

Shuming Zhao, Professor and Dean at China's Nanjing University School of Business and Dean of the School of Graduate Studies at Macao University in China, is an international specialist in human resources and multinational business management. He has published over twenty books and one hundred and seventy articles in his field and is a visiting professor and lecturer at various universities in the USA, Canada, UK, Germany, Holland, Australia, Japan and Singapore. Huifang Yang is a post-doctoral fellow at The Nanjing University School of Business.

Ervin Drake has credits both as a writer of Broadway shows like *What Makes Sammy Run* and *Her First Roman* and as a composer of popular music such as "It Was a Very Good Year," "I Believe," and "Quando, Quando, Quando." His songs have been recorded by Frank Sinatra, Barbara Streisand, Tony Bennett, Ray Charles, Willie Nelson and many other artists.

The Brothers Grimm, Jacob (1785-1863) and Wilhelm (1786-1859), were 19th century German scholars who published collections of legends and folktales, including such notables as "Cinderella" and "Rumpelstiltskin."

Clive Dunn is a British actor best known for his role as the elderly butcher in the late 1960s BBC comedy series "Dad's Army" and later as a similar character in a children's series called" Granddad." His song "Granddad" was number one in sales in Britain in 1971 and listed on the popular music charts for twenty-seven weeks.

Arnold Drake has written over 1500 graphic novel stories during his career, including *Batman, Superman, X-Men, Twilight Zone, Bullwinkle and Rocky, Little Lulu, Bugs Bunny,* and created *Doom Patrol* and *Deadman.* In 2005, he was the recipient of the prestigious Award for Excellence in Comic Book Writing.

Karol Josef Wojtyla served as the Roman Catholic Archbishop of Krakow Poland from 1964 to 1978 when he was elected Pope John Paul II. He died at age 85 in Rome Italy on 2 April 2005.

John Timperley was a financial services executive in the United Kingdom before becoming a playwright. His latest work, *Kennedy, The Thousand Days,* was recently staged in London.

Wynne Miller, niece of the famed American bandleader Glenn Miller, appeared on Broadway as Daisy Mae in *Lil Abner* as well as in *A Thurber Carnival* and *Tenderloin*. Her other credits include the films *The Way We Were* and *Annie* and the television series "Somerset" as well as many appearances on the Today and Tonight shows.

Rudolf Anton Bernatschke was born in Salzburg Austria and began learning his craft of portrait painting in Vienna and Paris before coming to America before World War II. Many celebrities have been painted by him, including Tom Wolfe, Chevy Chase, Ernest Hemingway, Gary Cooper, Cardinal Spellman among others.

Cao Qingyang was a chemical engineer before the Cultural Revolution forced him for seven years into farm and manual labor. He then served in the Chinese Ministry of Education and later became head of China'a Education and Science Press. He is currently Dean and Director of Beijing University College in China.

Hank A. Cepeda, from the Dominican Republic, is a noted computer graphics artist with an under-graduate degree in Fine Arts from The Parsons School of Design and a graduate degree from Brooklyn College.

About the Author

The late Professor Umberto Vasari presents from Rome fifteen authors from around the world who offer a philosophy or a viewpoint or an idea to help us grow older without growing old. From the happy acceptance of being older, shared with us by British novelist Richard Jones, through some timeless reflections about ageing by the elderly Polish Pope John Paul II to the lively prescriptions of a senior educator from China, Professor Cao Qingyang, the various authors show us in different ways the value and purpose of growing older. Also they teach us by word and by example the art of ageing.

978-0-595-38261-3
0-595-38261-4